Our
ALL-SUFFICIENT GOD

Beyond Suffering

In the

Book of Job

Leta A. Haggard

Carol Culp Robinson

This study is dedicated to Christian leaders and mentors who exemplify the character of Job. They look beyond their circumstances to our All-sufficient God and say with Job:

I have heard of You by the hearing of the ear;

But now my eye sees You.

—Job 42:5

This recent study of the ancient story of Job is packaged in such a way so as to maximize applications based upon several key principles that flow through the book's 42 chapters. It serves well as a guidebook enabling the reader to learn and to grow through a fresh interaction with the contents of Job. Although devotionally driven, it maintains a soundness in the crucial areas of hermeneutics and theology.

George J. Zemek, Th.D.
Academic Dean, the Expositors Seminary, Jupiter, Florida

Your study on the book of Job has brought to life the God I have come to know.

—Bible study student

After studying Job, I am much more careful in conversation to choose words that speak rightly about God.

—Bible study participant

More Comments

I believe that I have learned more about the character and sovereignty of God through this study than any other study I have participated in. I am truly humbled by the author's words and organization of the suffering of Job. My life and heart have been changed by seeing God in a new, greater way. I can trust that God is good and carries out His plans the best way . . . to bring Him glory.

I really enjoyed this study. It helped me see false thoughts I had regarding God's attributes and the truth of God's sovereignty. . .

Thank you for your efforts/service to the Lord in development of this study. It has been tremendously convicting, challenging and blessed in my life.

I loved how much depth in the scripture I had to dig for in this study.

I so appreciate these lessons. I feel such an intimate understanding of this book and it has had a wonderful impact on my life and my relationship with my Father in heaven. I think through this study God has helped me release some of my own grief. . .

CONTENTS

TABLES

FIGURES

INTRODUCTION

Is God in control over all?

Is God just?

Is God loving?

Is God all-knowing and all-wise?

The book of Job was written in the early stages of God's progressive revelation of Himself to man. Therefore, Job and his friends grappled with questions such as those listed above and their weighty implications. They were without specific knowledge of the coming of a Messiah who would redeem man from his sins, who would give meaning to life after death and who would act as a mediator between God and man. Yet Job longed for such a mediator (Job 9:33).

In the midst of his suffering, all Job had was faith in his God, whom he knew as the all-sufficient

God, Almighty God and bestower of fruitfulness. At times, this God-tested, enduring faith looked rough, crude and raw. Yet Job's faith in the all-sufficient God did endure. Through the experience, God revealed to Job, and subsequently to us, His attributes of majesty, sovereignty, providence, lovingkindness, justice, omniscience and wisdom.

We take this often neglected and overlooked book of the Bible, separate it from its usual theme of suffering and show the enduring truths of God's character. We believe the book of Job demonstrates that God is worthy to be loved, trusted, worshiped and served in all circumstances. Though the study addresses questions about evil and righteousness, the suffering of the righteous and the prosperity of the wicked, we maintain that the over-arching theme is the grandeur of our incomprehensible God.

Why the Individual Needs This Study

What we believe about God shapes our interpretation of God's dealings with us and with others and determines our actions. *Our ALL-SUFFICIENT GOD: Beyond Suffering in the Book of Job* invites the student to look beyond the clouds of suffering and circumstances. The student is encouraged to lift her eyes higher and higher, to see not only the hand of God, that is, what He does, but to see the face of God – who He is: His character as He reveals Himself in the book of Job.

The student can benefit from this study in the following ways:

1. She can gain an appreciation for the majesty of God and His sovereignty over the affairs of heaven and earth as well as His providential working of all events and happenings to accomplish His own purposes and pleasure.

2. She can know better God's character as presented in the book of Job and extolled in James 5:11: "You have heard of the endurance of Job and have seen the outcome of the Lord's dealings, that the Lord is full of compassion and is merciful."

3. She can learn to speak rightly about God as He cautions us to do in the book of Job.

4. She can develop the character of Job that pleases God, one who is "blameless, upright, fear[s] God and turn[s] away from evil" (Job 1:1).

5. She can be prepared to learn all that God wants to teach her when afflictions come to her.

As she participates in this study, the student will develop the following:

- word study skills
- a list of Job scriptures on the character of God
- comforting skills

- evangelism skills
- a firm biblical answer to the four questions posed at the beginning of this introduction
- right thinking about God when troubles come

May the Lord graciously use those afflictions to grant the student a deeper intimacy with Him, so that she can say with Job, "I have heard of You with the hearing of the ear; but now my eye sees You" (Job 42:5). Finally, we hope that this study will be a joy to the student and that she will delight in Who God is and not in just what He can do for her.

A Guide to Learning from This Study

Our ALL-SUFFICIENT GOD: Beyond Suffering in the Book of Job is designed as a 13-week, student-friendly study. It works well for individuals and for both small and large groups. Ideally, groups will need a leader or teacher or both, to teach and guide the group in discussing each week's material.

Week one requires no preparation on the student's part. The leader or teacher will kick off the group study by taking a look with you at the Introduction, which is rich with preparatory instructions, background and overview materials.

Weeks two through 12 are each divided into five days of study. Most days' assignments will average 30 minutes. They may include reading a passage from Job and answering questions about that passage. Cross-referencing—looking up other scriptures—is often used. Cross-referencing allows one passage of scripture to help interpret another passage, either from the book of Job itself or from another Bible book. Sometimes a word study may be assigned for clarification. However, the goal is not necessarily to fill in every blank. If you do not understand a question, relax and move on to the next one. The answer may become clear later. If not, bring up the question in your group time.

Begin each study session by asking God for insight. The assignments listed at the beginning of each day are there to help you to interact with God and His Word. The *italicized personal application questions* offer opportunity to move from observing and interpreting the text to applying it to your own life. Be alert to a special interview assignment from Lesson 11 Day 4. During the course of your study, think of a Christian woman who has endured a trial or test that resulted in a maturing intimacy with the Lord. Plan a time to interview her using the guide provided in Lesson 11.

You will begin *Our ALL-SUFFICIENT GOD: Beyond Suffering in the Book of Job* with the Introduction. There, in addition to being introduced to the four pivotal questions to be answered throughout this study, you will read about the following:

- Background. *Job: The Background* is plentiful in details about Job the man and the book of Job as a whole.
- Drama. *The LORD's Mysterious Dealings with Job* is a three-act play replete with a narrator and characters from the book of Job. It tells the story in earnest dialogue, a bit jazzed in appropriate places. Acted out or simply read through, the play provides an engaging way to view the book as a whole. It is recommended to present the play during the introductory group session or, as an alternative, immediately after Lesson 2 as a summary of the overview survey. Repeat the play on the last day of class. It will serve as a great review and reminder of how "real" God, Job, the friends and the events have become to you!
- Word studies. Looking up the meaning of a particular Hebrew word used in Job may be intimidating to a newcomer to word study. The Introduction includes *A Word about Basic Word Studies*, a simple "how-to".
- Charts on the attributes of God to be used in Lessons 6-12. As you may have guessed from its title, this study pivots on God—His dealings with Job, His mysterious ways and His attributes. In the Introduction, you will find charts along with an explanation of how to use them and definitions of God's attributes that are pertinent to the book of Job.

Chapter Summaries and Benefits to the Student

Lessons 1 and 2 center on the *Discovery Survey*, an overview of Job that will help the student develop a good grasp of the "big picture" and the chronology of events. Such an overview is essential as the rest of the study is more topical, although it does follow the general chronology of the book. The benefits of the survey are intrinsic; it guides the student to think and study from a God-centered perspective rather than centering on the man Job. It includes *Discovery Survey* charts to identify speakers, sections and themes. Each assignment ends with the opportunity for the student to evaluate her awareness of God's activity in her life.

Lesson 3 addresses the circumstances surrounding Job's losses. Specific losses include those of family and health, authority and fellowship and friends' support. The student is asked to evaluate her own personal losses and her response to adversity in her own life and in the lives of others.

Lesson 4 identifies problems related to comforting those in grief. The student must consider whether God's blessings and promises are absolute and if God's wisdom can be trusted. She will be challenged to assess her beliefs about God's role in suffering and prosperity. She will assess her own comforting skills and will devise an aid to comforters using Bible verses.

Lesson 5 scrutinizes Job's lifestyle as a God-fearer. The student will become sensitized to upholding God's reputation. She will evaluate her own integrity by comparing herself to Job. She will develop strategies for turning away from temptation and evil.

4

Lessons 6 through 8 highlight some of God's attributes that are displayed in the book of Job. **Lesson 6** offers a high view of God as all-sufficient and sovereign over the heavenly realm, the earthly realm and Satan. The student learns to appreciate God's providence in governing and sustaining creation and humans for His own purposes. The student also learns about God's provision for dealing with Satan. **Lesson 7** challenges the student to line up with scripture her beliefs about God's wisdom and omniscience, His nearness and transcendence and His justice. In studying Job's complaints against God's justice, the student must consider the justification for any complaint of her own against God's justice. **Lesson 8** continues the study of God's justice by exploring God's dealings with the wicked and the righteous. The student is challenged to practice active justice by obeying biblical commands to care for the poor and needy and to judge other Christians biblically.

Lesson 9 explores Job's response to suffering. The student will learn how to respond to God's dealings by trusting Him, reframing circumstances, praising God and seeking His wisdom and gaining an eternal perspective.

Lesson 10 explains the continuity from the Old Testament through the New Testament of God's great salvation by faith. The student will write an explanation of Old Testament and New Testament faith and will develop evangelism skills.

Lesson 11 gives Elihu's perspective on Job's suffering. The student will explore reasons for unanswered prayer. She will learn principles for interpreting suffering from a God-centered perspective. Through an assignment to interview a mature Christian who has endured troubles, she will understand how she can know the Lord more deeply through troubles. She will have the opportunity to "stand and consider the wonders of God" through an experiential assignment.

Lesson 12 relates God speaking to and restoring Job. This enjoyable climax to Job's trials gives the student an opportunity to see God afresh and to assess her pre-study thoughts and post-study thoughts about God and to identify the change.

Following the weekly material, the section entitled **Finale** validates the God-centered intent of the study. The section wraps up the answers to the four pivotal questions posed in the **Preface** that the student is to consider throughout the study.

Reflections, appearing at the end of most lessons, are weekly reviews designed for group use. The questions about each day's assignment facilitate discussion. *Reflections* may also be useful individually to evaluate your own understanding of the week's lesson.

JOB: THE BACKGROUND

There was a man in the land of Uz whose name was Job.

—Job 1:1

The Old Testament book of Job has fascinated Bible scholars through the centuries. When was it written? Who wrote it? Was Job a real person, or a product of imagination or perhaps a composite of all who suffer? Was Job a mythical hero, his story passed down by oral tradition?

Job, the Man

Most scholars agree that Job was an actual historic figure, although some want to place him in the parable category, similar to the good Samaritan or the prodigal son.[1] In other parts of scripture, Job is referred to as a real person, like Noah and Daniel: "Even though Noah, Daniel and Job were in its midst, as I live," declares the Lord God, "they could not deliver either their son or their daughter. They would deliver only themselves by their righteousness" (Ezekiel 14:20). Writing in the New Testament, James also considered Job to be real: "Behold, we count those blessed who endured. You have heard of the endurance of Job and have seen the outcome of the Lord's dealings, that the Lord is full of compassion and is merciful" (James 5:11).

Bible writers not only treat Job as a real man, but also one of his friends. The apostle Paul quotes Eliphaz in Job 5:13 as he wrote to the Corinthians: "For the wisdom of this world is foolishness before God. For it is written, 'He is the one who catches the wise in their craftiness'" (1 Corinthians 3:19).

For this study, the writers take the position that Job was an historical figure, his story inspired and written by God through a man for inclusion in God's Word for His purposes.

There are at least two possibilities for the meaning of the name *Job*. Author David Garland concurs with others who hold that Job is a derivative of a Hebrew term that carries the idea of "enmity," "the hated one" or "the persecuted one." Job may also come from an Arabic root which means "the penitent one."[2] Based on Job's character and how he responded when God finally confronted him, either meaning or both would be appropriate.

Job, the Historic Time Frame

Job probably lived in patriarchal days (roughly 2100-1700 B.C.), perhaps between the time of building the Tower of Babel and the time of Abraham's call by God, or a few years later.[3] Extrabiblical texts dated as early as 2000 B.C. refer to a Job, a common West Semitic name in the second millennium B.C. That name appears in a list of kings dating from 2000 to 1800 B.C., but there is no evidence that the biblical Job is included on the list.[4]

Job's lifestyle, his wealth measured in livestock and his role in the family mirror that of patriarchs Abraham, Isaac and Jacob. Job's length of life also corresponds to that of the patriarchs. Because his children were grown when calamity fell upon him, Job could have been about 60 years old then. After God restored all to him, Job lived another 140 years (Job 42:16). Other biblical figures who died "full of days" were Terah (Abraham's father) at 205; Abraham, 175; Isaac, 180; and Jacob, 147. In contrast, Joseph lived only to age 110, and men's lives thereafter have been shorter (Psalm 90:10).

Some writers give evidence for early dates of Job's life by pointing to the lack of references in Job to Hebrew institutions such as the law or to any events in the history of Israel. (Although there is mention of sacrifice, the burnt offerings of Job 1:5 are not Levitical offerings brought by the people and which only priests sacrificed.) Others say that Job and his friends were not Israelites, so there naturally would be no mention of anything Hebrew.[5]

Other evidence for the patriarchal age is that the book of Job refers to God as Shaddai 31 times and uses the Hebrew name for God, Jehovah, in the prose sections and only once in the poetry section (Job 12:9). The patriarchs, like Abraham, were familiar with Shaddai.[6]

Further persuasion for an early date lies with the Sabeans and Chaldeans, the people who raided Job's livestock (Job 1:15, 17). They early were nomads but became city dwellers in later years.[7]

Job, the Author?

Job could not possibly have written the book that bears his name, say some scholars. Why? Because Job never learned of the dialogue between God and Satan concerning him.

Bible scholars can only conjecture about who wrote the book. Perhaps it was Elihu, the fourth friend, who could have penned an eyewitness account. Jewish tradition holds that the writer was Moses because of several similarities between Job and Genesis, which is credited to Moses. Moses also lived for 40 years in the land of Midian, located adjacent to Uz.[8] Or perhaps the author was Solomon because of his interest in wisdom and poetic literature. The book of Job is included in the wisdom and poetic category along with Solomon's writings: Proverbs, Ecclesiastes and Song of Solomon.

For His own reasons, God did not choose to reveal the author, as He did not for the New Testament book of Hebrews.

Job's Home

The Book of Job places Job the man in the land of Uz. He probably was a native of Uz, specifically from an area called "the east" (Job 1:3). One writer has placed the region northeast of Palestine, near desert land (1:19), possibly between the city of Damascus and the Euphrates River. That area would fall today near the borders of modern Iraq and Saudi Arabia. Refer to the map in figure 0.1.[9]

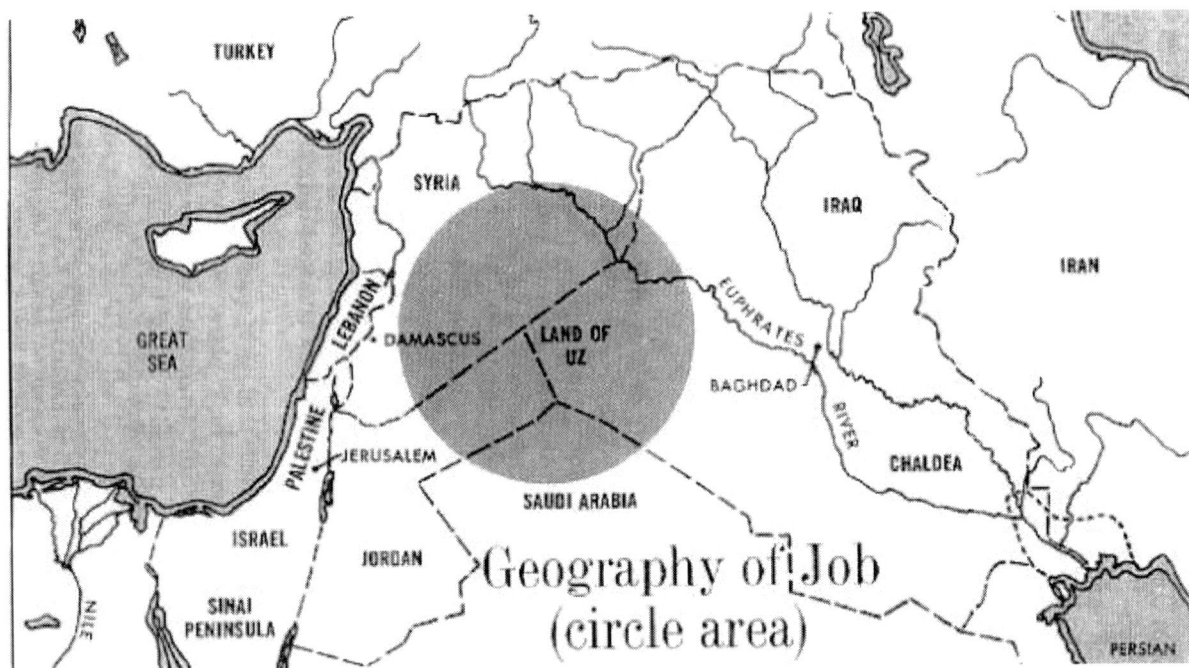

Figure 0.1. Map of Middle East and Possible Location of Uz

Uz is mentioned two other times in the Bible. Jeremiah 25:20 refers to Uz as a land of kings; Lamentations 4:21 says that Uz was a possession or neighbor of Edom. One author presents a case for Uz being located in an area of current northern Saudi Arabia or southern Jordan, which had been called Edom since the time of the Patriarchs.[10]

Uz could have been in Edom, southeast of the Dead Sea. The names of Job's friends and their homes also point to locales in the desert country east and south of the Dead Sea. Another locale might have been in the fertile Bashan, south of Damascus. Several verses in Job (1:3, 14, 19 and 42:12) place Job living in northern Arabia where land was fertile for agriculture and raising livestock. This location could have been Hauran, a region east of the Sea of Galilee. Most significantly, wherever Uz was located, it was outside Palestine, to the east or southeast. (NOTE: Palestine was a land area bordering the Mediterranean on its west; the name had no political overtones.)[11]

The Book of Job as Literature

The book of Job begins, *"There was a man . . ."* and ends, *"and Job died."* In between is what some have said is an epic poem penned by a master storyteller. Even in the world of secular literature, Job is recognized as a magnificent dramatic poem. It is quoted three times in the Burial Service of *the Book of Common Prayer.*[12] The great composer Handel included Job 19:25 in his wonderful work, *Messiah.*[13]

Job is the first of the poetical or wisdom group of Old Testament books. Others are Psalms, Proverbs, Ecclesiastes and Song of Solomon. Many of these are written in poetry. So is the entire book of Job except chapters one and two and most of 42.

Hebrew poetry does not rhyme, although some scholars debate whether or not it has meter like English poetry. All of Job's chapters except one and two and most of 42 are written in couplets, the second line or thought parallel to the first. The second line can echo the same sentiment as the first, or it might be antithetical. Sometimes couplets on the same subject or thought are put into groups of up to eight lines.[14]

As a student, do try to look at a Bible translation that lays out in poetical form the portions of Job which are written as poetry. And as you spend time reading Job for this study, purpose in your mind to appreciate the beautiful way the thoughts are expressed and connected.

This study of Job, *Our ALL-SUFFICIENT GOD: Beyond Suffering in the Book of Job*, does not explore the intricacies and difficulties of analyzing Job from the Hebrew nor as wisdom literature or poetry. The Book of Job (like the book of Isaiah) is replete with vocabulary words that appear nowhere else in the Bible and some that appear only a few times in the Old Testament.[15] Scholars have differed through the centuries upon how to interpret the book of Job from the original Hebrew language. We have chosen to use the *Updated New American Standard Version* of the Bible.[16]

The Names of God in the Book of Job

The Lord led us to write with an emphasis on God rather than on Job the man. How could we reflect that? The most obvious way was with a God-centered title. We researched to understand the names of God that He chose to include in His book.

Five names of God are used in the book of Job: **God, LORD, Lord, the Holy One and the**

Almighty. The names *God (#430 'elohiym)* and *LORD (# 3068 Yehovah or YHWH)* were mostly used in the prose section of the book of Job, while the names *God (#433 'elowahh* and *#410 'el)*, *Lord (#136)*, *Holy One (#6918 qadowsh)* and *Almighty (#7706 shaddai)* were used mostly in the poetry section, chapters three through forty-one. We will draw other beneficial conclusions from this knowledge later in the study.

Further research on combining the names *el* and *shaddai* elaborates upon God's ability to fulfill His promises. The *New Bible Dictionary* states that the Almighty, *El Shaddai* was interpreted by early Jewish commentators as "the all-sufficient."[17]

We can have confidence that God Almighty, *El Shaddai,* our all-sufficient God, is more than able to care for and satisfy His children. Job learned at the end of his trials that God is, indeed, all-sufficient to meet his every need: "I know that You can do all things, And no purpose of Yours can be thwarted. . . . I have heard of You by the hearing of the ear; but now my eye sees You" (Job 42:2, 5).

If Job, the most righteous man of his day who represents the ultimate sufferer, found that "the Lord is full of compassion and is merciful" (James 5:11), then we can trust God to be all-sufficient to take us through and beyond any and every kind of suffering we will ever face. Thus, we have entitled this study, *Our ALL-SUFFICIENT GOD: Beyond Suffering in the Book of Job.*

Blessed be the name of the LORD.

—Job 1:21

Notes

1. William Henry Green, *Conflict and Triumph* (Carlisle, PA: Banner of Truth Trust, 1999. Copyright 1999 by Banner of Truth Trust), 5.

2. David D. Garland, *JOB, A Study Guide* (Grand Rapids: Zondervan, 1971. Copyright 1971 by Zondervan), 12.

3. Irving L. Jensen, *Job* (Chicago: Moody, 1975. Copyright 1975 by Moody Bible Institute of Chicago), 8.

4. Garland, 12.

5. H. L. Ellison, *A Study of Job from Tragedy to Triumph* (Grand Rapids: Baker, 1958. Copyright 1958 by Paternoster), 17.

6. Roy B. Zuck, *JOB* (Chicago: Moody, 1978. Copyright 1978 by Moody Bible Institute of Chicago), 10.

7. Zuck, 10-11.

8. Zuck, 8.

9. Jensen, 7-8.

10. Robert L. Alden, *The New American Commentary: Job* (Nashville: Broadman and Holman, 1993. Copyright 1993 by Broadman and Holman), 29.

11. Lawrence O. Richards, *The Revell Bible Dictionary* (Old Tappan, New Jersey: 1990. Copyright 1990 by Fleming H. Revell), 753.

12. *The Book of Common Prayer* (New York: Henry Frowde, Publisher to the University of Oxford, 1892), 294, 298- 299.

13. George Frederic Handel, *Messiah*, Libretto, Part III.

14. Jensen, 12.

15. Zuck, 7.

16. *The Holy Bible Updated New American Standard Bible* (Grand Rapids: Zondervan, 1999. Copyright 1999 by Zondervan).

17. J. D. Douglas, ed., *New Bible Dictionary* (Wheaton: Tyndale, 1982. Copyright 1982 by Universities and Colleges Christian Fellowship, Leicester, England), 25-26.

THE LORD'S
MYSTERIOUS DEALINGS WITH JOB
A Drama in Three Acts

By Leta A. Haggard and Carol Culp Robinson

Cast of Characters

Narrator
The LORD Almighty
Satan, the evil one
Job, a man from Uz

Job's wife, Mrs. Job
Three friends of Job: Eliphaz, Bildad, Zophar
Elihu, a fourth friend of Job

Props
Large name placards for all nine characters
Electric fan
Broken piece of pottery (or substitute)

Act 1

The setting switches between heaven and earth. The LORD sits on his throne (preferably out of sight of the audience but close enough so that he can be clearly heard.) The electric fan prop is close enough to him so that he can turn it on later. Job is sitting to the far side praying. He has the pottery prop concealed. Satan stands facing the "invisible" LORD on his throne.

Narrator: *On earth, it is a hot, wind-driven day in the land of Uz. As far as the eye can see, Job's flocks and herds graze. His many servants scurry about as they cater to the greatest man of the east. Job has just finished offering a daily burnt sacrifice for his ten children. Job is devoted to God and wants His children to walk in God's ways.*

In heaven, God, the Ruler of the universe, has called a business meeting of His subordinates, and Satan has come along. God is going to put his servant, Job, on display.

LORD: Satan, have you considered my servant Job? Have you ever seen such devotion to Me in anyone else?

Satan: Oh, his devotion is only because of what You give him.

LORD: Test him out, then, and let's just see what happens.

Satan: He will curse You to Your face.

LORD: You can touch everything he has. Just don't touch him.

Narrator: *One by one, Job's servants bring him devastating news of marauding and natural disasters and the death of his children. Reeling from the barrage of late-breaking, heart-breaking news, Job tears his robe, shaves his head, falls to the ground and worships God.*

Job (kneels to pray): "Naked I came from my mother's womb, and naked I shall return there. The LORD gave and the LORD has taken away. Blessed be the name of the LORD." **(Job sits again.)**

Narrator: *At another business meeting in heaven, the LORD again puts Job on display.*

LORD: Have you considered My servant Job? Have you seen such devotion? I am pleased with the way he has handled all this devastation and has remained true to Me.

Satan: When it gets right down to a man's life, he'll do anything to save it. But if You take away his health, he'll fold and curse you to your face.

LORD: Give it your best shot, but you may not kill him.

Satan exits for good. Mrs. Job enters and stands over Job.

Narrator: *Pity poor Job. Look at him now, sitting on the town dung heap, covered in boils from head-to-toe. Using a lance common at the time, he is scraping his sores with a broken, sharp-edged piece of pottery. Along comes Mrs. Job.*

Mrs. Job to Job: Look at you! After all of this, are you still hanging on to your devotion to God? Curse God and die!

Job (sitting and scraping with pottery): You're talking foolishly, woman! Shall we accept good from God and not accept trouble?

Narrator: *Job does not take his wife's advice. He remains faithful to God. Scraping, scraping, scraping…*

Act 2

Narrator: *Job is now sitting alone on the dung heap. His wife has deserted him. His brothers and sisters and other relatives have deserted him. Instead of sitting as a judge at the town gate, he is the town outcast. Suddenly, three figures appear on the heat-blurred horizon. Job recognizes them as his friends—Eliphaz, Bildad and Zophar-- who live some distance away. But why are the men here? As soon as they get close enough to recognize him, they begin weeping loudly. They tear their robes and throw dust on their heads as if in mourning! They are so overcome by Job's appearance that they throw themselves down on the ground near him. They speak not a word for seven days and seven nights for they see that his pain is very great.*

Finally, Job breaks the silence.

Job, continuing to scrape with pottery: I curse the day I was born. I wish I could just die and be done with it all. What I feared has really happened. No peace and quiet, only trouble.

Narrator: *You would guess that the three friends would have wonderful, consoling words in response to Job's lament. After all, they have been sitting on the dunghill in anguish with him for a week. But, in their minds, they have jumped to conclusions about why Job is suffering. They don't hesitate to let him know exactly what they are thinking. Job responds in kind and argues his case before God.*

Eliphaz to Job: Job, you must have turned from God and lied about it for God to be punishing you so severely. Get right with God. Accept His discipline so you can get on with the good life.

Job: I have not denied the words of the Holy One! I am righteous **(Job points up to heaven in the direction of the invisible LORD.)** Watcher of men, quit watching my every move and pardon me instead!

Bildad: You've forgotten God. Seek Him. Be a man of integrity and He won't reject you.

Job: I am righteous and not guilty, but God judges me guilty. Look how He destroys the guiltless with the wicked. He mocks the despair of the innocent. He allows injustice even from the supreme court judges. **(Job looks up and points.)** Why do You condemn me and contend with me, yet look with favor on the guilty. **(Job lowers his head and hand.)** I'm not getting anywhere with God on my own. I need a negotiator.

Zophar to Job: God knows hypocrites. You talk too much! You are so self-righteous. Stop pretending and get real.

Job to friends: I know as much as you do and more. You don't have any idea how powerful God is over us and our circumstances. I will argue my case before God. **(Job points up.)** Stop the pain and dread of You! You overpower man and destroy his hope. But I'm waiting for better times when You and I will be friends again.

Eliphaz: Job, you are wicked in saying such things to God and fighting Him.

Job to friends: Sorry comforters! Is there no limit to your windy words! **(Job points up)** God, I'm so confused. At the same time that You are my Defender, You are my Enemy as well. And if that's true, what hope do I have? I'm already the talk of the town.

Bildad: You're winding up an angry wicked man who doesn't know God as you claim.

Job to friends: How wrong you are! I <u>do</u> know God and that He Himself has struck me. Even so, I'm sure that someone will eventually take up my cause. Someday I'll be back in good standing with

God.

Zophar shakes his head "no": NO! NO! Your troubles are pay-back for the way you've mistreated others.

Job: You're wrong about me. Just because a man has troubles doesn't always mean he's wicked. A wicked man can have a really good life. In the end, though, all the wicked end up dead.

Eliphaz: Say what you want! You're still a wicked man. You need to get right with God.

Job, sadly: What a nightmare! Everyone believes I'm guilty and God is nowhere to be found. Why doesn't God set things right in the world?

Bildad to Job: Are you questioning God's justice? You are forgetting that God is awesome and man is a maggot.

Job to friends: You are no help! God is powerful. He stretches out the north over empty space and hangs the earth on nothing. How can we understand His actions? We know that He <u>will</u> settle the score with wicked people. A wise man fears the Lord and cuts out wrong doing. I once was considered wise. Back when God watched over me, I was well-respected for my wisdom and advice. But now that God has afflicted me, people like you call me names and don't think twice about insulting me. God knows my integrity. Let the Almighty answer me!

Friend Elihu enters. He sits down with Job and the three other friends.

Narrator: *Well, after those furious rounds of debate, the flurry of trading insults, assigning blame and calling God's character into question, the three friends fall silent. There is nothing left for Job to hear! But wait. Who is this fifth man who begins to speak? Where did he come from? He is Elihu, a much younger man than the others. From his first words it appears that he has been privy to the entire debate. My, he certainly has a mouthful to say.*

Elihu to all: I am younger than you and was shy and afraid to tell you what I think. However, I've had a bellyful of your words. I will burst if I don't tell you my opinion. Here goes. I'm angry against you three for not finding any real answers for Job but for condemning him anyway. And I'm angry against you, Job, because you keep trying to justify yourself before God! You know, God often strikes down a man to keep him from pride and self-destruction. Confess to God your wickedness and rebellion. God does not do wickedness or wrong, but he breaks men who do. No man, righteous or wicked, has anything to give to God. It is God who gives to man. He opens ears so that man will learn to obey Him and thus prosper. Know, then, that God does not violate justice and righteousness. You say that you are eager to hear from God. Simply stand and consider the wonders of God, One perfect in knowledge.

All four friends exit the stage. Job stays on stage.

Narrator: *Now, be reverent because God, who has been silent throughout the debates, has chosen this particular moment to answer Job.*

Act 3

The LORD is still in His concealed spot. Job sits on the ground, facing the audience. The LORD turns on the electric fan and speaks loudly over the noise.

LORD to Job: Who is this spouting what he doesn't know? Now straighten up and act like a real man while I question you. Then you instruct Me, if you can.

Where were you when I laid the foundations of the earth? Tell ME, if you have understanding. Who set its measurements? Or who stretched the line on it? On what were its bases sunk? Or who laid its cornerstone when the morning stars sang together and all the sons of God shouted for joy? Who enclosed the sea with doors, when bursting forth it went out from the womb? Where were you when I laid the foundations of the earth? Tell ME, if you know all this.

Have you ever in your life commanded the morning and caused the dawn to know its place? Have you taken hold of the ends of the earth and shaken the wicked out of it? Have you entered into the springs of the sea or walked in the recesses of the deep?

Have you entered the storehouses of the snow, or have you seen the storehouses of the hail which I have reserved for the time of distress? Have the gates of death been revealed to you? Or have you seen the gates of deep darkness? Where is the way to the dwelling of light? And darkness, where is its territory? Can you bind the chains of the Pleiades or loose the cords of Orion? Do you know the ordinances of the heavens, or fix their rule over the earth?

Do you know the time the mountain goats give birth? Did you set the wild donkey free? Did you make the foolish ostrich? Did you give the horse his might and clothe his neck with a mane? Is it at your command that the eagle mounts up and makes his nest on high?

You, Job, are a faultfinder. Will you contend with the Almighty? Answer me.

Narrator: *Job is stunned. He has been begging God to answer him. Now that God does answer with words reflecting His might and power, Job can only manage three stumbling sentences.*

Job: "I am insignificant; what can I reply to You? I lay my hand on my mouth. Once I have spoken, and I will not answer; even twice, and I will add nothing more." **(Job puts his hand over his**

mouth and leaves it there.)

Narrator: *But God is not satisfied with Job's reply. He answers Job out of the storm. God's first words are familiar.*

God: Now straighten up and act like a real man while I further question you. Then you instruct Me if you can. Will you really annul My judgment? Will you condemn Me that you may be justified? If you have an arm like Mine and if you have a thundering voice like Mine, then you clothe yourself with honor and majesty like Mine. Then you can humble the proud and tread down the wicked where they stand. You do these things, and I will confess to you that your own right hand can save you.

Look at the mighty and fierce beasts of My creation, Behemoth and Leviathan. Are you sufficiently mighty that you can get close enough to Behemoth to capture him? Are you sufficiently brave enough to creep up on Leviathan and fill his skin with harpoons or his head with fishing spears? You can't stand before these beasts. Who, then, do you think you are to stand before Me?

Narrator: *Who, indeed, can answer such a challenge from the all-sufficient, majestic God? No one, including Job. This time he replies in true repentance.*

Job to the LORD (takes hand from mouth): I know that You can do all things and that no purpose of Yours can be thwarted. I confess that I have talked about things which I don't understand, things too wonderful for me which I did not know. **(Job looks up to heaven.)** I have heard of You by the hearing of the ear, but now my eye sees You. **(Job bows head humbly.)** Therefore, I despise myself and repent in dust and ashes.

The LORD turns off the fan. Eliphaz, Bildad and Zophar enter and stand facing the direction of the LORD.

LORD to Eliphaz: Eliphaz, My wrath is kindled against you and your two friends because you have not spoken of Me what is right, as My servant Job has. Now take seven bulls and seven rams and go to My servant Job. Offer up a burnt offering for yourselves. My servant Job will pray for you, for I will accept him so that I may not do with you according to your folly, because you have not spoken of Me what is right as My servant Job has.

Job stands and discards pottery. The three friends take the offering to Job. Job prays silently for them. Then the three friends exit the stage.

Job is alone on the stage, facing the audience. He lifts face and both arms to heaven.

Job: The LORD has doubled my wealth. He has given me ten more children. My brothers and sisters and friends are socializing at my house again. The LORD has blessed my latter days more than my beginning. I have learned that in good times or in bad times, God is still worthy to be praised.

ALL THE CAST: Blessed be the name of the LORD!

THE END

A WORD ABOUT WORD STUDIES

The book of Job as well as most of the Old Testament was written in Hebrew. Therefore, we will study some Hebrew words to better understand the meaning of the text. Because responsible Bible study views the text itself as the primary source of study, looking at a particular word is always done in context.

In your homework assignments, you have been supplied with the reference numbers for research on words used in *The Holy Bible Updated New American Standard Bible*.[1] Those reference numbers are the same as in the *Strong's Complete Word Study Concordance*.[2] Get to know the resources at your fingertips in the exhaustive concordance. They include the following:

1. *Strong's* Concordance in alphabetical order for looking up words from the Bible. You will find lists of phrases with every occurrence of the word in the whole Bible, along with chapter and verse and its reference number.

2. *Strong's* Hebrew and Greek Dictionaries that list words by reference number, giving their English translation and how many times a definition is used.

Various editions of *Strong's Concordance* exist, with varying amounts and depth of information provided. Other resources for word studies include an expository dictionary, which elaborates upon the definition of some Bible words. *Vine's Expository Dictionary of Biblical Words*[3], commonly used, is keyed with the *Strong's* reference numbers. The *Hebrew-Greek Key Word Study Bible*[4] includes a built-in word studies section for quick and easy reference. For the computer-literate, Bible software is available which includes various Bible versions, exhaustive concordances and commentaries. It actually makes word studies fast and fun!

Notes

1. *The Holy Bible Updated New American Standard Bible* (Grand Rapids: Zondervan, 1999. Copyright 1999 by Zondervan).

2. *Strong's Complete Word Study Concordance* (Chattanooga, TN: AMG, 2004. Copyright 2004 by AMG).

3. *Vine's Complete Expository Dictionary of Old and New Testament Words* (Nashville: Nelson, 1985. Copyright 1985 by Thomas Nelson).

4. Spiros Zodhiates, *Hebrew-Greek Key Word Study Bible* (Chattanooga, TN: AMG, 1990. Copyright 1984 and 1990 by AMG).

ATTRIBUTES OF GOD CHARTS
FOR LESSONS 6 – 12

In keeping with our emphasis on God as you study the book of Job, you will be guided in the practice of identifying the various characteristics or attributes of God as they appear in Scripture.

Theologian Wayne Grudem wrote, "Although God's power is infinite, his use of that power is qualified by his other attributes (just as all God's attributes qualify all his actions)."[1] Grudem warned that misunderstandings of God's attributes result if one attribute is isolated from the rest of God's character or is in any way overemphasized or underemphasized.[2] With that caveat, for the purpose of this study, you will consider God's attributes using six broad categories:

- God's all-sufficiency
- God's sovereignty, omnipotence and providence
- God's justice and righteousness
- God's wisdom and omniscience
- God's incomprehensibility and transcendence
- God's lovingkindness

The *Attributes of God* charts in figures 0.2 through 0.4 are useful tools for gaining insight into who God is. Definitions of the attributes are provided. Throughout the study, be alert for the following:

- ❖ Beginning in Lesson 6, be alert for God's attributes as they are emphasized in scripture.
- ❖ Check the assignment box daily for reminders to write on the charts. Record insights and scriptures meaningful to you.
- ❖ Personalize the charts as your very own treasure. Enjoy sharing them with your study group.

Your compilation will be indispensable for the final lesson. At the end of the study, you will have a composite with some of God's wonderful attributes to treasure and refer to in the future.

Notes

1. Wayne Grudem, *Systematic Theology* (Leicester, England: Inter-Varsity, 1994. Copyright 1994 by Wayne Grudem), 217.

2. Grudem, 217.

ATTRIBUTES OF GOD

God's All-sufficiency

God is self-sufficient and does not need man.
God is unaffected by man's wickedness or man's righteousness,
yet He cares for man.
God gains nothing from us, yet He desires a relationship with us
and has provided the means for that relationship.

God's Sovereignty, Omnipotence and Providence

God's sovereignty means that God rules over all and controls all things.
God's omnipotence is His ability to rule.
God's providence is His active involvement in governing and sustaining His creation
for His own plans and purposes.

Figure 0.2. Attributes of God charts for God's all-sufficiency and sovereignty, omnipotence and providence

ATTRIBUTES OF GOD
God's Justice and Righteousness God is always just and right in all He does. His justice is undeviating and abundant. God is the righteous, impartial Judge. God is jealous for His name.
God's Wisdom and Omniscience God knows how to bring about His plan. God knows and does what is best. God is omniscient or all-knowing, perfect in knowledge. Nothing is hidden from God.

Figure 0.3. Attributes of God charts for God's justice and righteousness and wisdom and omniscience

ATTRIBUTES OF GOD
God's Lovingkindness God is concerned for His creation, granting and preserving life. The Lord is full of compassion and is merciful.
God's Incomprehensibility and Transcendence God is incomprehensible so that we are not able to fully understand His nature, character and ways. This is also called the inscrutability of God. God is transcendent. He is self-sufficient and beyond His creation.

Figure 0.4. Attributes of God charts for God's lovingkindness and incomprehensibility and transcendence

DISCOVERY SURVEY: STRUCTURE AND THEMES

LESSONS 1 and 2

Can you discover the depths of God? Can you discover the limits of the Almighty [all-sufficient One]?

—Job 11:7

No, we cannot discover the depths and limits of limitless, all-sufficient God. But God, through His dealings with His servant Job, chose to reveal to us *"mysteries from the darkness"* and to bring *"the deep darkness into light"* (Job 12:22). What joys await you as you discover for yourself truths about God, His ways and His Word from the book of Job!

<u>Your study goal for the first two weeks is to gain a firm grasp of the entire book</u>. Making that goal easy are a guided survey for daily reading and a companion Discovery Survey featured in tables 0.1 and 0.2:

- The guided survey is divided into two lessons of ten days, five per week. Each day's assignment specifies scripture portions to read and questions to answer. The questions are designed to help you find the themes (the main ideas) of those chapters.
- First, you will read daily the assigned chapters and answer the questions.
- Second, you will transfer one or more answers of your choice to the Discovery Survey in tables 0.1 and 0.2.
- Table 0.1 is divided into three columns: (1) sections (2) chapters and (3) speaker(s). The first two columns—sections and chapters—are filled out for you. The two explain the chronological unfolding of God's discussions with Satan, rounds of debate among Job and his four friends and God's response. In column 3 you will record the speakers for each segment. On table 0.2, record one or more main ideas that you choose from your answers to the daily questions, as explained above. (Optional: Color code each speaker with his main ideas.) The finished Discovery Survey will be a very helpful reference tool for the remainder of the study.

Remember to ask the LORD, our All-sufficient God, for insight each day, perhaps with the following prayer adapted from Job 23:12: "LORD, help me to understand and treasure your Word more than my necessary food."

Table 0.1 Discovery survey sections, chapters and speakers

DISCOVERY SURVEY		
Section	Chapter	Speaker(s)
Contest between God and Satan	1-2	*God, Satan, Job, Mrs. Job*
First Round of Debate	3-10	
	11-14	
Second Round of Debate	15-17	
	18-21	
Third Round of Debate	22-25	
Job's Final Defense	26-31	
Elihu Defends God	32-37	
God Responds	38-41	
God Restores Job	42	

Table 0.2 Discovery survey themes

DISCOVERY SURVEY
Themes (Main Ideas)
Lord allows Satan to test Job.

LESSON 1 SURVEY

Day 1—Survey: The Contest

I have treasured the words of His mouth more than my necessary food.
—Job 23:12

Assignment: 1. Read chapters 1 and 2.
2. Answer the questions.
3. Record one or more main ideas on the Discovery Survey in tables 0.1 and 0.2.

The first two chapters of Job introduce all but one character (Elihu) of the book. You will meet God and listen in on His challenge to Satan. You will meet Job, whom God calls "upright." You will meet Job's servants and his family, including his wife, who speaks two sentences and then is not heard from again. Note the dialogue, which reflects some of the major themes of the book.

1. How did the LORD describe Job to Satan?

   1:8

2. The LORD allowed Satan to afflict Job for what purpose?

   1:9

3. The LORD allowed Satan to afflict Job in what ways?

   1:14-19; 2:7

4. Satan twice predicted Job's response to loss. The first of Job's responses was to the loss of his family and possessions. What was Satan's prediction?

1:11

5. What was Job's response to loss?

1:20-22

6. The second of Job's responses was to physical suffering. What was Satan's prediction of His response?

2:5

7. What was Job's response?

2:10

8. At the end of **chapter 2**, what does Job know about the conversation between God and Satan?

9. At the end of **chapter 2**, what does Job know about the cause of his suffering?

As you complete each day's assignment in Lessons 1 and 2, use figures 1.1 through 2.5 to write your personal insights.

MORE THAN MY NECESSARY FOOD

After completing this assignment , I am aware that God

Figure 1.1. More than My Necessary Food awareness exercise

Day 2—Survey: First Debate, Chapters 3-10

I have treasured the words of His mouth more than my necessary food.
—Job 23:12

Assignment: 1. Read chapters 3 through 10.
2. Answer the questions.
3. Record one or more main ideas on the Discovery Survey in tables 0.1 and 0.2.

Chapter 3 begins the first round of debate between Job and Eliphaz, Bildad and Zophar. You will see Job weeping over the fact that he was ever born. His three friends, who had silently mourned with him, now have much to say. Listen for their explanations of his suffering.

1. Chapter 3 begins the debate between Job and three of his friends. What did Job curse?

3:1

2. The first friend to break the silence was Eliphaz the Temanite. What did he infer about Job?

4:7, 8

3. What did Eliphaz advise Job to do?

5:8

4. How did Job respond to Eliphaz's advice?

6:10, 29

5. What was Job's complaint to the "watcher of men"?

7:19-21

6. What did Bildad, the next friend who speaks, advise Job to do?

8:5-6

7. What did Bildad infer about Job?

8:20

8. How did Job respond to Bildad's advice?

9:20

9. What did Job accuse God of doing?

9:22-24

10. What would Job like to say personally to God?

10:2, 3

MORE THAN MY NECESSARY FOOD

After completing this assignment, I am aware that God

Figure 1.2. More than My Necessary Food awareness exercise

Day 3—Survey: End of First Debate, Chapters 11-14

I have treasured the words of His mouth more than my necessary food.
—Job 23:12

Assignment: 1. Read chapters 11 through 14.
2. Answer the questions.
3. Record one or more main ideas on the Discovery Survey in tables 0.1 and 0.2.

This section completes the first round of debate. Zophar joins Eliphaz and Bildad in rebuking Job, who sharply answers his critics. Job's prayer from 13:20 through chapter 14 is a lament in which Job begins to build his case before God.

1. What did Zophar, Job's third friend, infer about Job?

11:4-6, 11

2. What did Zophar advise Job to do?

11:13, 14

3. What was Job's response to Zophar?

12:3

4. What did Job say all nature knew that his friends did not know?

12:7-9

5. Cite some examples Job gave of God's power over nature and man.

12:13-25

6. What was Job's plan?

13:3, 15

7. What outcome to his plan did he expect?

   13:18

8. In Job's lament, he asked God to do two things. What were they?

   13:20-21

9. Next, in **14:14**, what hope did Job express?

10. Finally, of what else did Job accuse God? (**14:19-20**)

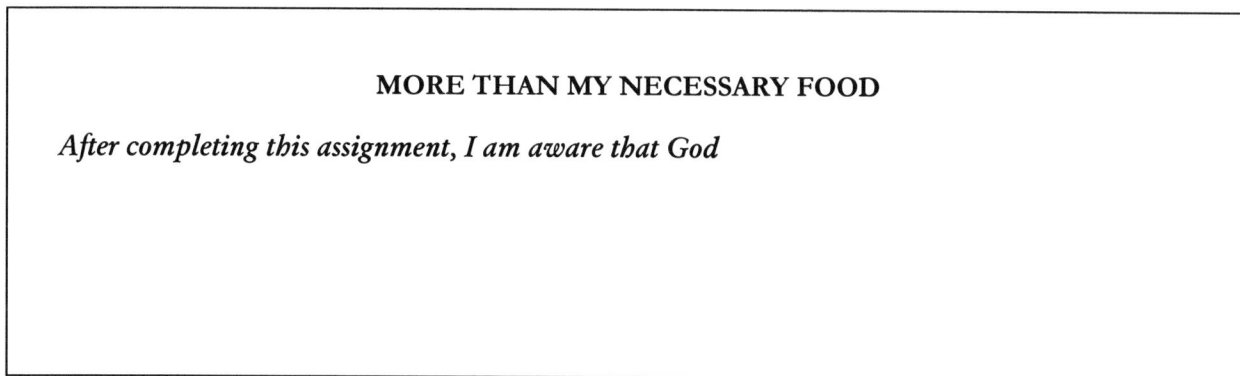

MORE THAN MY NECESSARY FOOD

After completing this assignment, I am aware that God

Figure 1.3. More than My Necessary Food awareness exercise

Day 4—Survey: Second Debate, Chapters 15-17

I have treasured the words of His mouth more than my necessary food.
                                                                —*Job 23:12*

Assignment: 1. Read chapters 15 through 17.
2. Answer the questions.
3. Record one or more main ideas on the Discovery Survey in tables 0.1 and 0.2.

The second round of debate begins in chapter 15 and ends in chapter 21. Watch today as Eliphaz's dialogue reflects the friends' increasingly mean-spirited, hostile and accusatory tone. Job retorts by calling them "sorry comforters" and lashing out at God.

1. According to Eliphaz, by what was Job condemned?

   15:6

2. Of what did Eliphaz accuse Job in **15:13?**

3. How did Eliphaz describe the fate of the wicked?

   15:20

4. What was Job's opinion of his three friends at this point in the dialogue?

   16:2, 20

5. What did Job call God? **16:9, 19**

6. What was Job's spiritual condition in **17:1?**

7. What did Job ask from God in **17:3?**

8. What had happened to Job's reputation and who did he blame?

   17:6

9. Job's spiritual outlook further darkened. What did he lose?

   17:15

MORE THAN MY NECESSARY FOOD

After completing this assignment, I am aware that God

Figure 1.4. More than My Necessary Food awareness exercise

Day 5—Survey: Second Debate Ends, Chapters 18-21

I have treasured the words of His mouth more than my necessary food.

—Job 23:12

Assignment: 1. Read chapters 18 through 21.
2. Answer the questions.
3. Record one or more main ideas on the Discovery Survey in tables 0.1 and 0.2.

Bildad and Zophar insult Job further by describing the wicked man, who in their minds looks a lot like Job. They do not hesitate to tell Job that he is getting what he deserves and reaping what he sowed—the fate of the wicked. Job begs for pity instead of persecution.

1. How did Bildad identify Job?

   18:4-5

2. Bildad peppered Job with many examples of bleak circumstances facing the wicked man. List three of them from **chapter 18**.

3. What was Bildad's final assessment of a wicked man?

   18:21

4. How did Job respond?

   19:1-3

5. What did Job insist had happened to him?

   19:6

6. What did Job ask from his friends and why?

   19:21

7. What confidence did Job voice in **19:25-26?**

8. Zophar identified Job as a wicked man and accused him of what specific sins?

20:19

9. What was Job's retort to Zophar's accusations against him?

21:27, 34

10. What did Job believe to be the fate of the wicked?

21:23-26

MORE THAN MY NECESSARY FOOD

After completing this assignment, I am aware that God

Figure 1.5. More than My Necessary Food awareness exercise

LESSON 2 SURVEY

Day 1—Third Debate, Chapters 22-25

I have treasured the words of His mouth more than my necessary food.
—Job 23:12

Assignment: 1. Read Job chapters 22 through 25.
2. Answer the questions.
3. Record one or more main ideas on the Discovery Survey in tables 0.1 and 0.2.

Zophar abstains from the third debate. Eliphaz and Bildad mock Job and accuse him of specific sins. The two urge him to repent from unrighteousness and return to God. But Job bemoans God's seeming distance from him and indifference to the wicked.

1. Of what great wickedness did Eliphaz accuse Job in **22:5-9**?

2. What did he urge Job to do?

   22:23

3. Why did Job want to find God?

   23:3-5

4. How did Job express his faithfulness to God?

   23:11-12

5. What was Job's condition that he attributed to God?

   23:16

6. List three of the many wrongs that Job thought God ignored.

24:1-16

7. According to Job, what happens to the wicked after they are exalted a little while?

24:24

8. What was Bildad's assessment of God?

25:2

9. What was Bildad's assessment of man?

25:6

MORE THAN MY NECESSARY FOOD

After completing this assigment, I am aware that God

Figure 2.1. More than My Necessary Food awareness exercise

Day 2—Job's Final Defense, Chapters 26-31

I have treasured the words of His mouth more than my necessary food.
— Job 23:12

Assignment: 1. Read Job 26 through 31.
2. Answer the questions.
3. Record one or more main ideas on the Discovery Survey in tables 0.1 and 0.2.

Job's monologue is covered in six chapters. The language is beautiful and descriptive as he reflects on God's greatness, reminisces about his own past glories and laments his current state. He defends his own righteousness, searches for true wisdom and proclaims his integrity.

1. In chapter 26, over what does God have power, according to Job?

26:6-13

2. How did Job answer his friends' accusations of wrongdoings?

27:5-6

3. How does God's portion (recompense) of the wicked man affect the wicked man's children, wealth and security?

27:14-22

4. Job asked in **28:12**, "Where can wisdom be found? And where is the place of understanding?" How did he answer his own question?

28:28

5. Job lamented as he contrasted his present circumstances with the past. What was his lifestyle when God watched over him?

29:6-17

6. What was Job's lifestyle now that God "has afflicted me"?

30:9-17

7. What did Job consider to be the portion and heritage of the Almighty toward the wicked?

31:2-3

8. Job ended his dialogue by dramatically declaring his integrity with a long list of wicked acts he had avoided and by calling down judgments upon himself if he had ever committed falsehood, lust, greed, idolatry or theft. What judgments did he declare for himself for such acts?

31:8-11, 22, 28, 40

9. What did Job cite as deterrents to wickedness?

31:14, 23

MORE THAN MY NECESSARY FOOD

After completing this assignment, I am aware that God

Figure 2.2. More than My Necessary Food awareness exercise

Day 3—Elihu Defends God, Chapters 32-37

I have treasured the words of His mouth more than my necessary food.

—Job 23:12

Assignment: 1. Read Chapters 32 through 37.
2. Answer the questions.
3. Record one or more main ideas on the Discovery Survey in tables 0.1 and 0.2.

Elihu has evidently been listening to the debate. Now the young upstart speaks his opinion. Elihu eagerly defends God as he acts as a transitional figure between Job and his three friends and God.

1. Against whom did Elihu's anger burn and why?

    32:2-3

2. What reasons did Elihu give for God opening men's ears and sealing their instructions?

    33:16-18

3. What was Elihu's advice to Job?

    33:26-27

4. How did Elihu defend God?

    34:10-12

    35:12

    35:14

5. Elihu included Job with the evil men of **34:37** and **35:12**. Of what did he specifically accuse Job?

6. In question 2 of today's assignment, you discovered reasons why God opens men's ears. Elihu gave more reasons in **36:10-12, 15**. What are they?

7. What did Elihu urge Job to do?

    37:14

8. What did Elihu call God?

    37:16

9. Elihu ended his dialogue with a glowing portrait of awesome God. What did he say?

    37:22-24

MORE THAN MY NECESSARY FOOD

After completing this assignment, I am aware that God

Figure 2.3. More than My Necessary Food awareness exercise

Day 4—God responds, Chapters 38-41

I have treasured the words of His mouth more than my necessary food.
—Job 23:12

Assignment: 1. Read Job 38 through 41.
2. Answer the questions.
3. Record one or more main ideas on the Discovery Survey in tables 0.1 and 0.2.

Until now God had been silent. "Then the LORD answered Job out of the whirlwind, and said, 'Who is this that darkens counsel by words without knowledge? Now gird up your loins like a man and I will ask you, and you instruct Me!'" (38:1-3).

1. In a series of over 80 questions God rebuked Job using examples from His creation. What examples of His power did God use to instruct Job?

   38:4, 19, 24-26, 32; 39:1, 27

2. From **chapters 38** through **41**, what are some of your favorite examples from God's instruction? List several below and include the references.

3. In the midst of questioning Job, the LORD said, "Will the faultfinder contend with the Almighty? Let him who reproves God answer it." What was Job's answer?

   40:3-5

4. Next, "the LORD answered Job out of the storm." He repeated His previous instructions: *"Now gird up your loins like a man; I will ask you, and you instruct Me."* But this time, He had added words for Job. What were they?

40:8-9

5. The LORD, as Owner of the universe, used two of his mightiest creatures as an example of His own power. What two creatures did he ask Job if he could tame?

40:15; 41:1

MORE THAN MY NECESSARY FOOD

After completing this assignment, I am aware that God

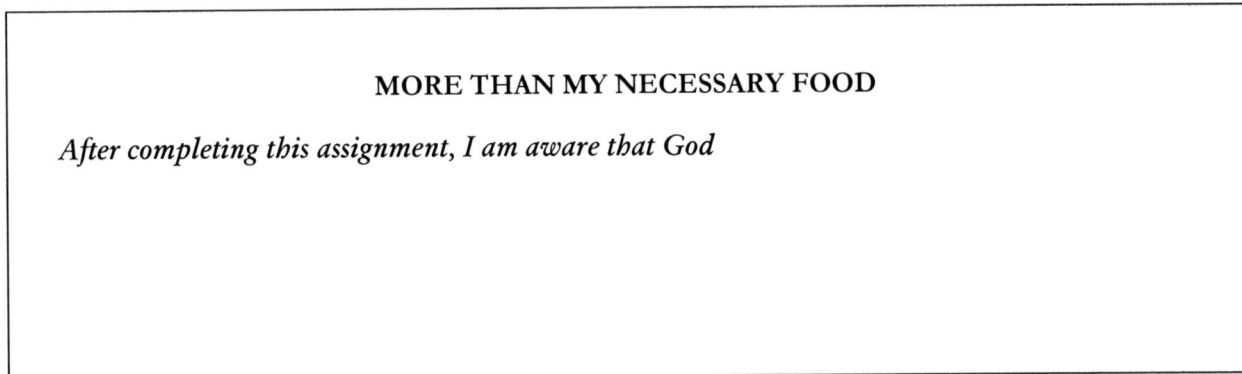

Figure 2.4. More than My Necessary Food awareness exercise

Day 5—God Restores Job, Chapter 42

I have treasured the words of His mouth more than my necessary food.
—Job 23:12

Assignment: 1. Read Job 42.
2. Answer the questions.
3. Record one or more main ideas on the Discovery Survey in tables 0.1 and 0.2.

Job cannot instruct God! Instead, he repents in dust and ashes. God commends Job for <u>now</u> speaking rightly about him, but rebukes Eliphaz, Bildad and Zophar. The intimacy with God for which Job longed is restored beyond his expectations. Answer the following questions from your reading of **Job 42**.

1. What did Job learn about God?

2

What did Job realize about his own understanding?

3

2. What did Job realize about his relationship to God?

   5

3. After Job saw God for Who He was and himself for who he was, what did he do?

   6

4. What was God's judgment against Eliphaz, Bildad, and Zophar?

   7-9

5. The LORD restored the fortunes of Job in what way?

   10

6. How did Job end his days?

   12a, 16-17

MORE THAN MY NECESSARY FOOD

After completing this assignment, I am aware that God

Figure 2.5. More than My Necessary Food awareness exercise

"…You have seen the outcome of the Lord's dealings, that the LORD is full of compassion and is merciful." (James 5:11b)

Congratulations on finishing your survey of the book of Job!

Now that your Discovery Survey is completed, review it often. In future lessons you will discover the details of the main ideas. Having the Discovery Survey will help you as our all-sufficient God "reveals mysteries from the darkness, and brings the deep darkness into light" (Job 12:22).

REFLECTIONS ON LESSONS 1 AND 2

Truths I have learned that deepen my relationship with the Lord

Review the major divisions of the book of Job.

Discuss your favorite *More Than My Necessary Food* in figures 1.1 through 2.5.

LESSON 3 JOB'S LOSSES

Day 1—Circumstances

Through all this Job did not sin nor did he blame God.

—Job 1:22

Assignment: Read Job 1 and 2.

Consider the Discovery Survey you have completed and declare it a good friend. Hopefully, the book of Job's less-read chapters have now united with the more familiar prologue and epilogue to provide a welcome big picture of the Lord's mysterious dealings with Job. As you settle into the study, pop open a pair of proverbial binoculars. God's dealings deserve close scrutiny.

The book of Job opens with a description of a man in the land of Uz, who becomes the central figure in a contest between God and Satan. Five times in chapters 1 and 2 the setting switches between heaven and earth. At the end of chapter 2, other characters are introduced.

1. How was Job characterized?

   1:1, 3; 2:3

Describe Job's possessions.

What spiritual service did Job do for his sons?

How often did Job perform this service?

What is your primary petition to the Lord for your children?

Are you faithful to continually ("all the days") intercede for them?

2. "Now there was a day when the sons of God came to present themselves before the LORD and Satan also came among them" (1:6).

What was the first question the LORD asked Satan?

1:7

What was Satan's flippant response?

1:7

Next the LORD asked Satan <u>THE</u> question on which the contest between them hangs. What was <u>THE</u> question?

1:8

Scoffing, Satan answered back. What did he say about the Lord's relationship with Job?

1:9, 10

"But," said Satan, "put forth

1:11

What was the Lord's reply?

1:12

3. Summarize the first assault on Job.

1:13-19

What did Job do after he learned of these terrible losses?

1:20

Record Job's words as he worshiped.

1:21

"Through all this Job did not sin nor did he blame God" (1:22). To what does "all this" refer?

4. In a second encounter with God, Satan said that Job had not yet reached the breaking point. What was his reasoning? **2:4**

What was Satan's solution to break Job?

2:5

The LORD gave Satan a permission and a restriction. What were they?

2:6

Satan went out from the presence of the Lord to do what?

2:7

5. Job was sitting among ashes, scraping himself with a potsherd, when his wife offered her advice. What did she say?

2:9

Did Job agree with her? What was his reply?

How can you guard your thoughts and tongue when your husband or a friend asks your opinion?

6. "In all this," what did Job NOT do?

2:10

7. At this point, three of Job's friends entered the picture (**2:11-13**). In a short summary, tell who they were, why they came to see Job, and what they did.

Day 2—Health and Family

Behold, he is in your power, only spare his life.

—Job 2:6

Assignment: 1. Review Job 1 and 2.
2. Read selected passages.

Sovereign God allowed Satan to reduce Job from being the greatest of all the men of the east to a boil-scraping outcast of the town dung heap. Job's losses were grievous: his children, servants and property; his health; his wife's support; his lofty, prestigious standing in the community and beyond; and, most painful of all, his fellowship with God.

Today you will learn more about his losses in the areas of family and health, tomorrow about his losses of authority and fellowship. As you study, consider the words of Jesus Christ to a large crowd going along with Him: "If anyone comes to Me, and does not hate his own father and mother and wife and children and brothers and sisters, yes, and even his own life, he cannot be My disciple" (Luke 14:25-26). Imagine what your reaction might be in the face of devastating changes in your own life. Oh, that others might say about us the same as was said of Job: "Through all this Job did not sin nor did he blame God...Job did not sin with his lips" (Job 1:22, 2:10).

1. Wicked Satan was sorely disappointed with Job's steadfast worship of the LORD (Job 1:21). Below, write his retort to the LORD from **Job 2:4-5** (see yesterday's assignment).

2. What was the LORD's reply?

2:6

"Skin for skin!" Satan declared. What had he meant by that? Several explanations are available for that peculiar term. In early history skins were a most valuable property. Another idea is that "the term skin is also used to denote the person of a man generally (Job 18:3) and hence the proverb 'skin for skin' is in plain English 'property for person.'"[1] Another possibility is that the saying might be the equivalent of "an eye for an eye and a tooth for a tooth." A fourth implication is that until a man's own life is threatened, he has not been fully tested. So in Satan's view, Job still had not met the ultimate challenge. "All that a man has he will give for his life," he challenged. "Let me touch his bone and flesh and he will curse You to Your face."

God allowed Satan to strike Job with sore boils "from the sole of his feet to the crown of his head." That brief description only launched the boatload of physical suffering for Job. It is not pleasant to read about his physical symptoms, but it is necessary to understand the magnitude of them and his reactions to them.

3. Write in table 3.1 Job's afflictions. They combine to present two foul portraits, one visible to others, one experienced only by Job.

What a repulsive image greeted anyone who cared enough to look on Job! According to some scholars, the disease that transformed him may have been smallpox. Or because his limbs were swollen and black and his skin wrinkled like an elephant, he could have had elephantiasis. A Hebrew word translated "boils" was used to denote one of the ten plagues in Egypt (Exodus 9:8-11, Deuteronomy 28:27) and of King Hezekiah's illness (2 Kings 20:7).[2]

Table 3.1 Job's afflictions

JOB'S AFFLICTIONS	
Visible	**Experienced only by Job**
2:12	3:24
3:25	7:5
16:16	19:17
19:20, 33:21	30:17
30:27	30:30

4. By now, Mrs. Job, who does not appear again in the book, had voiced advice to her husband: "Curse God and die." Her husband wasted no time in answering. What did he say about her?

   2:10

For his answer, Job has been called "the best husband in the Bible" by some. Others say his answer was abrupt, insulting and full of rebuke. Whichever, he did rebuke Mrs. Job for <u>talking</u> as one of the foolish women, not for <u>being</u> a foolish woman. No one knows exactly what specific foolish women Job had in mind. The Hebrew word for "fool" used in Job 2:10 denotes moral corruption, impiousness and vileness (Psalm 14:1).

5. Some historians are hard on Mrs. Job; some are lenient. With which opinion (s) below do you agree? Mark your answers with an **X**.

   a. Mrs. Job had a lapse of faith.   _____

   b. Mrs. Job was just expressing her own misery.   _____

   c. Mrs. Job was angry with God and simply wanted Him to get on with what she saw as inevitable.   _____

d. Mrs. Job blamed her husband for the loss of her children and earthly goods.   _____

e. Mrs. Job was truly sympathetic, not wanting her husband to suffer anymore.   _____

f. Mrs. Job thought Job was as good as dead, so he might as well provoke

God to strike him dead.   _____

Can you speculate on any other reasons for Mrs. Job's harsh words to her husband, either positive or negative?

Do your words to your husband (or wife) reflect a kindness that is rooted in faith and confidence in the Lord?

What changes do you need to make to ensure a God-pleasing response in the face of adversity?

Have you known someone who has suffered a devastating loss, yet stood firm in faith throughout? Share below by describing the person and what happened. (Perhaps that person is you.)

The author of the book of Job did not choose to tell readers anything else about Mrs. Job. There is not enough information to know if she was the mother of Job's second set of children. But as Job sat in physical misery on the dung heap, he surely felt deeply the separation from his wife. First his children, servants and livestock—gone! Next, his wife's companionship and support.

What more could he lose?

Day 3—Authority and Fellowship

And that man was the greatest of all the men of the east.

—Job 1:3

Assignment: Read Job 29 and 30.

"What more could he lose?" Those words ended your study yesterday. Satan had made good on his ugly deal to take away all that Job had and all that he held dear. Then Satan had afflicted Job's body. Sovereign God had not allowed Satan to kill Job, but inherent in Satan's wicked actions were consequences that would tear at Job's pride and cripple his fellowship with God.

1. In **Job 2:8**, where do we find Job sitting?

In the following verses, what do you find associated with ashes?

2 Samuel 13:19

Esther 4:1, 3

Daniel 9:3

Jonah 3:6

What is the last word Job uttered in this book?

42:6

The ashes Job sat among were outside the city, part of the town dump that accepted both garbage and human waste:

> The dung . . . is carried in baskets in a dry state to that place outside the village, and there generally it is burnt once a month. If a place has been inhabited for centuries, the *mezbele* (garbage heap) attains a height far greater than that of the place itself. The rains of winter reduce the layers of ashes to a compact mass, and gradually convert the *mezbele* into a solid hill of earth. There lies the outcast who, smitten by loathsome disease, is no longer admitted to the dwellings of men. . . There lie the dogs of the village, gnawing perhaps some fallen carcase [sic] such as is often thrown there.[3]

2. There on the refuse heap sat Job. It is possible that he had dwelt on the heap for months (7:3) before his three friends showed up. Lonely and rejected by his brothers and sisters and all who had known him before (42:11), he probably had not chosen to live in the garbage dump. Instead, the site was most likely forced on him by his fellow citizens because of his woeful physical condition. Separated from family and friends, he had an abundance of time to think, to mourn what used to be, to lament his losses, to compare the past with the present. The verses from **Job 29 and 30** in table 3.2 reveal some of Job's lament, his assessment of his importance in the community before and after tragedy laid him waste. This assessment is important because its veracity is attacked later in the book. Look up the verses from **Job 29 and 30** and record your findings in table 3.2.

Job, once the "king" of his community, was now a laughingstock. He summed himself up in **Job 12:4.** Write his opinion.

Have you ever felt like an "outcast" from your family or church family? How did your feelings affect your view of God?

What pain and sorrow Job felt over his domestic losses! How keenly he felt the blow to his pride over loss of prestige in the community! But how secondary those losses were to his anguish over loss of fellowship with God!

Table 3.2 Job's self-assessment

JOB'S SELF-ASSESSMENT			
JOB 29		**JOB 30**	
Verse	**Job's standing <u>before</u> affliction**	**Verse**	**Job's standing <u>after</u> affliction**
7		1	
8			
9		8, 9	
10		10	
11			
12		15	
14			
15			
16		16	
21			
25			

3. "Where are you, God?" he demanded. Fill in the blanks below to complete **Job 29:2-5**, which begins his pitiable lament over his past relationship with the LORD.

"And Job again took up his discourse and said, 'Oh that I were _____ gone by, as in the days when _____me; When His _____shone _____, and by His _____ I _____darkness; As I was in the _____ of my days, when the _____of God was _____; When the _____ was yet with me.'"

4. Immediately, Job moved from speculating on his glorious past in the LORD to accusing Him of mistreating him. From **chapter 30**, what were some of his complaints?

11

19

21

22

What is his fear, his "knowledge," that God is going to do to him eventually?

23

Lest we are tempted to judge Job harshly, remember that we readers have information that Job did not. We know that God initiated the contest between Himself and Satan. We know that God did not afflict Job but that He allowed Satan to do so. We know that God, for His reasons, chose Job to be a test case because of his godliness. We know that Job passed the first two tests and defeated Satan. Perhaps Job was, as has been surmised, a man most honored. Will Job remain faithful? Will we?

Day 4—Credibility

Remember now, who ever perished being innocent? Or where were the upright destroyed? According to what I have seen, those who plow iniquity And those who sow trouble harvest it.

—Job 4:7-8

Assignment: Read selected scriptures.

What we believe about God shapes our interpretation of God's dealings with us. It is crucial to have a right opinion of God when blessings or adversities come. Otherwise, we will forget Him, curse Him or misinterpret His dealings with ourselves or others. We will see today and tomorrow that such misinterpretation can lead to harsh treatment of others.

Three friends of Job—Eliphaz the Temanite, Bildad the Shuhite and Zophar the Naamathite—had firm opinions of God when they arrived on the scene. Some of their ideas were correct, but of others God said, "you have not spoken of me what is right" (Job 42:7). In trying to explain Job's suffering, they defended God, His character and His works, but they did so through human reasoning. They failed to allow God to be sovereign in doing as He wishes with His creatures. They concluded that God had nothing to do with Job's suffering; therefore, the fault must lie in Job.

The friends had a well-established retribution theology of sowing and reaping: If you sow sin, they reasoned, you will reap God's punishment and if you sow righteousness, you will reap God's rewards in this life. Their staunch adherence to a distorted view of God's justice and rewards and their subsequent misapplication of it to Job's situation caused them to speak wrongly about God and Job. In their eyes, Job lost all credibility.

1. Eliphaz declared in **Job 4:7-8**: "Remember now, who ever perished being innocent? Or where were the upright destroyed? According to what I have seen, those who plow iniquity And those who sow trouble harvest it." Refer to these verses to answer the following three questions.

Upon what evidence did Eliphaz base his knowledge of sowing iniquity and harvesting trouble?

What did Eliphaz declare about the innocent and the upright?

Who harvests trouble, according to Eliphaz?

In **Job 22:5**, if a person harvests trouble, what would Eliphaz declare about him?

But what was God's estimation of Job, according to **Job 2:3**?

God validated Job's innocence, yet Job harvested trouble. Because Eliphaz based his judgment on what he had seen, he was wrong in his charge against Job; his skewed idea of God's justice and rewards allowed no other conclusion.

How often do you base your thoughts about God and His ways upon what you have seen or experienced as Eliphaz did in 4:8?

Upon what are you to base your opinion of God?

2. How is retribution theology validated in **Galatians 6:7-8**?

The "sow-and-reap" principle is biblical. Yet it cannot be held rigidly and absolutely. We must also recognize God's eternal judgment, as retribution and rewards may not be meted out in this life (2 Corinthians 5:10).

3. As Eliphaz falsely condemned Job, he failed to consider another strong and valid biblical principle: Not everything we harvest in life is the result of something we have sown. Identify and write the exceptions below.

Leviticus 19:9-10

Matthew 6:26

John 4:38

4. Jesus gave one of the clearest teachings in the Bible about an exception to Eliphaz's view on sowing and reaping. Read **John 9:1-3** about what occurred one day while Jesus was walking. Who did Jesus see? What question did His disciples ask Him?

What answer did Jesus give?

5. If God gave us the punishment we deserved, who could stand? Copy **Romans 6:23** for the most comforting exception to Eliphaz's sow-and-reap principle.

Thank God for giving you the eternal life that you do not deserve as a free gift through Jesus Christ.

Day 5—Friends' Support

Will you keep to the ancient path which wicked men have trod?
—Job 22:15

Assignment: Read selected scriptures.

Have you ever been falsely accused of sin so tenaciously that you wondered if it would be better just to confess to the false allegations and be rid of the issue? Surely such an option would be even more tempting if you were promised material blessings as a result. But Job would not budge from his declaration of his innocence and integrity. Thus his friends resorted to harsher and harsher words and allegations as the dialogue progressed. Job realized keenly the withdrawal of their support.

1. As you read the following scriptures, note the barrage of criticism leveled at Job by his friends.

    5:1-2

    8:2

    11:3

    15:5-6

Eliphaz even accused Job of crushing the helpless and "keeping the ancient path of the wicked" (Job 22:6-15).

How might you respond under similar circumstances to such a volley of criticism?

2. Job's friends resorted to destructive name-calling and personal attacks. Instead, how does **Galatians 6:1**

advise us to admonish one another?

With what goal?

With what caution?

Name two ways you could improve on the three friends' approach in correcting a friend.

3. Job's friends diagnosed his problem without knowing all the facts. What was that diagnosis in **22:4-5**?

Confident of their conclusion, the friends failed to consider God's sovereignty, presumed to know God's mind and used their own wisdom to speak for God. Job's agony in having to listen to their stinging attacks was compounded by their misapplied admonishment. What advice did the three give Job?

5:17

8:5

11:13-14

22:21-24

His friends' misdiagnosis led them to a wrong prescription: repent and be restored. When falsely accused, we must often remain quiet and wait upon the Lord to vindicate us. Though he had lost the support of his friends, how did Job express anticipation in **23:10** that he would be vindicated by the only One whose opinion really mattered?

Can you recall a time when someone advised you to repent of something for which you knew you were innocent? Did you try to defend yourself? What did you do to think and speak correctly about God and your relationship with Him? How might Job's example help you?

REFLECTIONS ON LESSON 3

Truths I have learned that deepen my relationship with the Lord

Day 1

By the end of chapter 2, despite his terrible losses and physical suffering, Job did not sin or blame God. What do you think Job recognized about God that kept him from sin?

What do you know about God that would keep you from sin?

Day 2

Describe Job's tangible losses.

If you have suffered similar losses, how did your responses compare to Job's?

Day 3

Tell about Job's life as an outcast.

Day 4

Give *examples* from your own experience or the experience of others of the biblical concept of sowing and reaping.

Give *exceptions* from your own experience or the experience of others of the biblical concept of sowing and reaping.

Day 5

Discuss the risks of presuming to know God's activity in your or another person's life.

Notes

1. Jerome H. Smith, *The New Treasury of Scripture Knowledge* (Nashville: Nelson, 1992. Copyright 1962 by Jerome H. Smith), 550.

2. Roy B. Zuck, *JOB* (Chicago: Moody, 1978. Copyright 1978 by Moody Bible Institute of Chicago), 18.

3. Franz Delitzsch, *The Book of Job*. Quoted by H. L. Ellison, *A Study of Job from Tragedy to Triumph* (Grand Rapids: Zondervan, 1958. Copyright 1958 by Paternoster), 26-27.

LESSON 4 COMFORTER

Day 1—Absolute Blessings or God's Wisdom?

If you return to the Almighty, you will be restored; if you remove unrighteousness far from your tent.

—Job 22:23

Assignment: Read Psalm 91 and other selected passages.

The assignments of Lesson 4 address the challenges comforters and counselors face as they minister to sufferers. Do they depend more on the prevalent thinking of the day rather than on God and His Word? Today you will discover that Job's comforters, Eliphaz, Bildad and Zophar, applied their retribution doctrine of sowing and reaping in rigid terms, not only to the punishment of the wicked, but also to the blessings of the righteous. They argued that God always blesses the repentant. Their counsel in general is true. The mark of wisdom literature is its instructional nature according to the way life tends to go. But their error laid in holding to the tenets of retribution theology in an absolute manner that "assumes an automatic connection between one's material and physical prosperity and one's spirituality." [1]

Bildad prophetically offered Job an incentive for repentance: Repent and God will restore your righteous estate. Your end will increase greatly (Job 8:20-22). Eventually, Job's estate <u>did</u> increase two-fold! Zophar listed such spiritual benefits of repentance as a brighter life, hope, steadfastness and secure rest (Job 11:15-19). Eliphaz urged Job to "Acquaint now thyself with him [God], and be at peace: thereby good shall come unto thee" (Job 22:21 KJV). Matthew Henry called this verse "good counsel though built upon a false supposition that Job was a wicked man. Yet the counsel is good for us all." [2]

1. In Job 5:17-26, Eliphaz advised Job to not despise the discipline of the Almighty, and then gave him

examples of blessings that would result from repentance. His speech in **Job 5:17-26** parallels **Psalm 91** in several ways. Match the ideas from **Psalm 91** with the following verses.

"From six troubles He will deliver you, even in seven evil will not touch you" (Job 5:19).

Psalm 91:3, 9-10

"In famine He will redeem you from death, and in war from the power of the sword" (Job 5:20).

91:5-7

"You will be hidden from the scourge of the tongue, and you will not be afraid of violence when it comes" (Job 5:21).

91:5-6

"For you will be in league with the stones of the field, and the beasts of the field will be at peace with you" (Job 5:23).

91:11-13

"You will know that your tent is secure, for you will visit your abode and fear no loss" (Job 5:24).

91:9-10, 14

"You will come to the grave in full vigor, like the stacking of grain in its season" (Job 5:26).

91:16

2. What encouraging blessings in both Job and Psalm 91! But are the promises absolute, as the friends insisted? Satan misused the promises of Psalm 91 when he tempted Jesus in the wilderness. In Matthew 4:1-11, Satan urged Jesus to throw Himself off the roof of the temple to prove He was the Son of God. The Scripture Satan quoted was Psalm 91:11-12 (see above). How did Jesus handle Satan's distortion of those verses? Jesus countered by "handling accurately the word of truth" (2 Timothy 2:15). What did He say in **Matthew 4:7**?

Author John Piper cautions about the inaccurate use of Psalm 91. That caution can also apply to our use of repentance's promised blessings in the book of Job. He warned not to use Psalm 91 the way Satan used it with Jesus, as promises without exceptions or qualifications:

I urge you to follow Jesus' interpretation of Psalm 91, not Satan's. That is, in your Gethsemane of suffering, pray for deliverance according to God's sovereign power and mercy (twelve legions of angels could have rescued Jesus, Matthew 26:53). But then say, "Not my will but thine be done." And believe that what befalls will not, in the end, be evil for you, but good (Romans 8:28).[3]

God always respects true repentance, yet we cannot define the terms of that respect or its application to this present life. Even though God honored Job's genuine repentance with forgiveness, restored fortune and ten more children, God did not resurrect Job's first set of children. Nor could Job be compensated for the pain and suffering he had endured. It is here where we enter into the mysteries of God. We cannot define blessings and promises any further and must trust in God's superior wisdom.

3. How does **Isaiah 55:6-9** reinforce the lesson that God honors genuine repentance in His own way far beyond our ability to understand?

Finally, we must trust God's wisdom rather than assume absolute blessings:

The book of Job does not deny the general rule, found repeatedly in the Scriptures, that God blesses the righteous. Instead, it says that the principle is not invariable, that God by His sovereignty can withhold— or bestow—His blessings as He chooses for purposes known only to Him.[4]

What do you do when you reach the limits of your own understanding?

Day 2—Reward or Relationship?

Why is light given to a man whose way is hidden, and whom God has hedged in? . . . For what I fear comes upon me, And what I dread befalls me.

—Job 3:23, 25

Assignment: Read selected passages.

You have learned from studying God's ways with Job that righteousness does not always result in showers of blessing. The book of Job "rejects any formula that affirms that the righteous always prosper and the wicked are always destroyed. There may be other reasons for suffering; rewards (of blessing or of destruction) may be long delayed; knowledge of God is its own reward." [5]

Without allowing for any other possibilities, the health, wealth and prosperity movement of our day has perverted the retribution theology. It claims that passages such as those you have studied in yesterday's lesson teach that God wants all of His children to be materially prosperous in this life and that success is an outward indication of God's favor upon a person. Its proponents have labeled their false teaching "name it and claim it" and "positive confessions." The "positive confessions" teaching is a belief that if you speak something, it will happen, placing power in man's spoken word rather than the written Word of God.

1. Read **Job 3:23-26** and consider the context of verse 25 in which Job stated, "What I fear comes upon me and what I dread befalls me." Bible students disagree about how to interpret this verse. Some say Job had anticipated trouble during his season of prosperity and the trouble he dreaded finally arrived. Others believe that in his prosperity Job realized that trouble eventually comes to all. In that way he was prepared to respond to troubles in the noble way he did in chapters 1 and 2. A popular teaching today is that Job did not practice "positive affirmations" but allowed negative thoughts which came true. If he had had only positive thoughts, they say, trouble would not have come. Please beware of such man-centered false teaching.

Perhaps the key to interpreting **3:25** is to keep it in context with **verse 23**. How does Job describe God's activity in his life?

Now read **Job 1:10** and notice what Satan said about God's hedge. Write it here.

The hedge that once protected Job now encroached upon him, hindering his relationship with God. Such a sense of disruption of fellowship would be deplorable to a God-fearer such as Job, thus eliciting a response of fear and dread. Robert Alden commented that in connecting Job 3:25 with Job 1:10, "we learn that hedges can make one feel safe and protected or fearful and threatened. In both instances it was God who put the hedge around Job." [6]

Is there a sense at this time in which you recognize that God has placed a "hedge" around you? What response does it elicit from you?

How can the "hedge" be used to draw closer to God?

2. Teachers of "name it and claim it" hold Bible promises as absolute and tend to neglect teachings in the Bible that are contrary to their view, thus creating a false and perverted view of the Christian's relationship with the world. Write what the following passages say rightly about:

- the power and purpose of the Word of God (**Hebrews 4:12**)

- the weakness and limits of man's words and intentions (**James 4:13-16**)

- the love of the world (**1 John 2:15-17**)

- the love of money (**1Timothy 6:9-10**)

- caring for the needs of others (**James 2:14-17**)

- suffering with Christ (**Romans 8:16-18**)

- having an eternal perspective (**Colossians 3:1-4**)

Have you had a distorted view of any of the above principles? If so, which one?

What steps do you need to take to correct your view?

Day 3—Cliché or Kindness?

For the despairing man there should be kindness from his friend; so that he does not forsake the fear of the Almighty.

—Job 6:14

Assignment: Read selected scriptures.

When Eliphaz, Bildad and Zophar first laid eyes on their ravaged friend Job, they reacted appropriately. They grieved with Job, sitting on the dung hill in silence for seven days. How welcome their arrival must have been! How comforted Job must have felt by their silence! All others close in proximity had deserted him, yet these three men had somehow heard about his sorrow, agreed to "come to sympathize with him and comfort him" (Job 2:11) and traveled a distance to be with him.

Stunned upon seeing Job, they went through the customary mourning rituals for the dead (Job 2:13, Genesis 50:10, I Samuel 31:13). The three friends saw that Job's pain was very great (Job 2:13), and they waited for him to break the silence. When he did (Job 3), their ensuing "comfort" was not what Job had probably anticipated.

1. In addition to accusations and calls to repentance, Job's friends questioned his faith in God. How did Eliphaz question that faith in **4:3-6**?

Apparently, Eliphaz considered his own words to Job synonymous with "the consolations of God" (15:11). Yet his words were anything but consoling!

> And the appeal to Job's piety, as though this should have quieted his clamour and led him still to maintain a cheerful hope amidst his overwhelming distress, showed a want of consideration for the condition in which he then was. There was in all this a lack of that tenderness and that appreciative sympathy which was a prime requisite in one who would comfort such a mourner as Job.[7]

Read **Job 6:14** at the beginning of today's study. What does a despairing man expect from his friend? Otherwise, what might happen to the despairing man?

2. Several times Job the griever tried to teach his friends how to be kind in comforting him: "Listen carefully to my speech and let this be your way of consolation" (Job 21:2). What comfort did Job want from his friends?

> **Job 13:5-6, 13-17**

> **Job 21:2-5**

3. What did Job give his friends permission to do in **6:24**?

With what limitations in **6:25-26**?

4. In **13:12** what kinds of "memorable sayings" and answers did Job decry?

> *Identify some maxims and platitudes that we insensitively use today with those who have experienced loss.*

5. Job reasoned that if their roles were reversed, he could take two approaches in comforting the friends. What were those two approaches?

> **16:4-5**

6. How does Job define vain comfort in **21:34**?

> *Have you heard or given any statements of false and vain comfort? Explain.*

Day 4—Self-centered or Word-centered?

But it is still my consolation, And I rejoice in unsparing pain, That I have not denied the words of the Holy One.

—Job 6:10

Assignment: Read selected passages.

When comforting others we often feel inadequate. We are! Sometimes we are anxious because we do not know what to do when a friend undergoes trials. We do not want to compound the suffering. Neither do we want to intrude. We fear saying the wrong words. It is right and proper that we should feel inadequate to comfort in our own ability. God wants Christians to depend upon Him when called upon to comfort because <u>He</u> is the Source of all comfort (2 Corinthians 1:3). Otherwise, we might become self-centered "miserable comforters" like Eliphaz, Bildad and Zophar who depended upon their own knowledge, experience, traditions and beliefs. Today's study focuses on the value of God's Word in comforting others.

[God] who comforts us in all our affliction so that we will be able to comfort those who are in any affliction with the comfort with which we ourselves are comforted by God.

—2 Corinthians 1:4

1. According to this verse, why does God comfort us in all our afflictions?

God enables us to comfort people who are in what type of affliction?

How does God enable us?

A common misconception is that to be effective, a comforter should have experienced the very same loss or trauma as the sufferer. While it can be helpful for the sufferer to talk with someone who has been in the same situation, 2 Corinthians 1:4 shows that, for the Christian, any true comfort originates from the Father of mercies and flows through the Christian to others.

2. When God calls us to comfort others, what will He do?

Isaiah 50:4 (a Messianic prophesy, but applicable to us)

Hebrews 13:21

2 Thessalonians 2:16-17

3. Identify from the following scriptures the value of remaining Word-centered in comforting others.

2 Timothy 3:16-17

Hebrews 4:12

4. One lesson from the book of Job is that God judges counselors who rely upon human wisdom instead of upon God and His Word. Identify from **Job 12:17-24** how God can deal with self-centered counselors by filling in the blanks below.

12:17 [God] makes counselors _____ _____ [a sign of humiliation] . . .

12:20 He _____ the trusted ones of speech and takes away the _____ of the elders.

12:24 He _____ of _____ the chiefs of the earth's people and makes them _____ in a pathless waste.

They _____ in darkness with no _____ , And He makes them _____ like a drunken man.

5. Even the most sincere human comfort has limitations. Our best friends can sometimes fail us in times of trouble, as Job's friends failed him. But God will never fail to comfort his children because He has promised that He will never leave us nor forsake us (Deuteronomy 31:6).

Complete the following Word-centered statements that describe God's comfort.

In **Psalm 23:4**, God's comfort is like

In **Psalm 94:19** God's comfort delights

In **Psalm 119:50** God's comfort in affliction is in

In **Psalm 119:52** God's comfort is found

In **Isaiah 49:13-16** God's comfort is toward

In **Isaiah 66:13** God's comfort is like

In **Jeremiah 31:12-14** God's comfort can turn

Identify a time when, in your despair, God was your only comfort. What scriptures or hymns were especially meaningful to you?

What did you learn from the experience that will make you a Word-centered comforter?

Day 5—Woeful or Hopeful?

Where now is my hope? And who regards my hope?

—Job 17:15

Assignment: Complete the *Aid To Comforters* chart located in table 4.1.

You have learned that Job's friends' comfort was inadequate and even harmful. They lacked compassion as Job lamented over his physical and spiritual deterioration. Like Job, a Christian may need help putting his theology into practice when difficulty comes. The *Aid to Comforters* chart in table 4.1 is designed to help Christians rightly comfort as they assist a suffering friend to move from comfortlessness to *"consider[ing] it all joy when you encounter various trials"* (James 1:2-4). After you have thoughtfully completed the chart, you can use it as a reference to offer hope. You can use God's Word in the same way an "antidote" would be used to offset poison in someone's system and to bring them to health.

The *Aid to Comforters* chart has four columns.

- **Column 1** lists scripture references which you will look up.
- **Column 2** is blank. In it you will record Job's complaints from the Scriptures in Column 1. The first one is filled in for you.
- **Column 3** lists summarized Bible verses to counter each complaint.
- **Column 4** is blank for you to fill in your ideas of practical ways to give hope with God-honoring comfort. An example is provided.

Table 4.1 Aid to comforters

AID TO COMFORTERS			
Reference	**Job's Complaints**	**Scriptural Antidote**	**Practical Ways to Give God-honoring Comfort**
Job 3:24; 6:6-7	*Loss of appetite*	Acts 2:42, 46 They met together and shared, prayed, worshiped. Matthew 25:35, 45 Do all as unto Jesus. Is. 8:13 Let Lord of hosts be your dread and fear	*Example: Take a meal to a hurting friend.*
Job 3:25-26		2 Timothy 1:7 (KJV) God has not given us a spirit of fear, but of power and of love and of sound mind. Isaiah 26:3 The steadfast of mind You will keep in perfect peace, because he trusts in You.	
Job 6:2; 18:4		Psalm 34:4 I sought the LORD and He delivered me from all my fears. Philippians 4:6-7 Be anxious for nothing . . . let your requests be made known to God, and the peace of God . . . will guard your hearts. Ephesians 4:26 Be angry but do not sin . . . do not delay dealing with it.	
Job 6:3; 7:11		Psalm 37:8 Cease from anger . . . do not fret, it only leads to evildoing. Philippians 2:14 Do all things without grumbling or disputing.	

Table 4.1 Aid to comforters, continued

AID TO COMFORTERS			
Reference	Job's Complaints	Scriptural Antidote	Practical Ways to Give God-honoring Comfort
Job 6:4		Hebrews 13:5 God will never leave nor forsake you. Psalm 94:14 The LORD will not abandon His people.	
Job 6:14; 7:6-7		Psalm 27:13 I would have despaired unless I had believed that I would see the goodness of the LORD in the land of the living.	
Job 6:15		Psalm 27:10 Though my father and mother forsake me, the LORD will take me up. Isaiah 53:3 Jesus our suffering Servant was despised and rejected.	
Job 7:3-4, 14		Proverbs 3:24 When you lie down, you will not be afraid, but will sleep. Psalm 4:8 In peace they will lie down and sleep. There is safety in the LORD.	
Job 23:2		Job 1:21 The LORD gave and the LORD has taken away. Blessed be the name of the LORD. Philippians 4:11 I have learned to be content in all circumstances.	

REFLECTIONS ON LESSON 4

Truths I have learned that deepen my relationship with the Lord

Day 1

What are some ways that we might overreach in our effort to explain God's activity in a person's life?

Day 2

What errors do some people make in holding to the retribution theology without qualification or exception?

Day 3

What did the three friends do wrong in their efforts to comfort Job?

How is God's comfort different from that of the friends?

Day 4

How does God empower us to comfort others?

List three things you have learned that will help you to better comfort those who are afflicted. Which of these is the hardest for you to do?

Day 5

How can you use information in table 4.1, "An Aid to Comforters" chart, to help a sufferer move steadily from despair to "count it all joy" (James 1:2)?

Notes

1. Walter A. Elwell, ed., *Baker Theological Dictionary of the Bible* (Grand Rapids: Baker, 1996. Copyright 1996 by Baker), 417.

2. *Matthew Henry's Commentary of the Whole Bible* (Peabody, MA: Hendrickson, 1991. Copyright 1991 by Hendrickson), 701.

3. John Piper, *A Godward Life: Book Two* (Sisters, OR: Multnomah, 1999. Copyright 1999 by Desiring God Foundation), 55.

4. Roy B. Zuck *JOB* (Chicago: Moody, 1978. Copyright 1978 by Moody Bible Institute of Chicago), 189.

5. D. A. Carson, *How Long, O Lord?* (Grand Rapids: Baker, 1990. Copyright 1990, 2006 by D. A. Carson), 155.

6. Robert L. Alden, *The New American Commentary: Job* (Nashville: Broadman and Holman, 1993. Copyright 1993 by Broadman and Holman), 79.

7. William Henry Green, *Conflict and Triumph* (Carlisle, PA: Banner of Truth Trust, 1999. Copyright 1999 by Banner of Truth Trust), 62.

LESSON 5
JOB: A GOD-FEARER'S LIFESTYLE

Day 1— Blessing God

Blessed be the name of the LORD.

—Job 1:21

Assignment: 1. Review *A Word about Basic Word Studies* located in the *Introduction*.
2. Refer to a concordance and /or a Bible dictionary.

What is it to bless God or to curse Him? Today we will answer the following questions:

- What did Job mean when he said, "Perhaps my sons have sinned and cursed God in their hearts"?

- What did Satan mean in tempting Job to curse God to His face?

- What did Job's wife mean in telling Job to "curse God and die"?

- What does it means to bless God?

1. Read **Job 1:5, 8-12** and **2:3-6, 9**. Use a study tool to look up the Hebrew word for "curse" (#1288) and its definition in these verses.

Barak, as meaning "to bless" occurs 330 times in the Bible, and is used only six times to denote profanity, four of those occurring in the first two chapters of Job.[1] Why then, was the word *barak* used to mean "to curse" when its overwhelming use is "to bless"? Matthew Henry, considering the Jewish thought of that day, suggested that "cursing God is so impious a thing that the holy language" would not permit its use.[2] Therefore, a euphemism was used. *The New Treasury of Scripture Knowledge* conjectures that "the primitive

Hebrew text was changed from *kalal,* 'to curse,' to *barak,* 'to bless,' out of reverence for the name of God." [3] Though there is no textual evidence to support such a claim, use of the euphemism highlights just how serious a crime it is to *kalal* or curse God.

Write the third commandment of Mosaic Law from **Exodus 20:7**.

The act of cursing God, called blasphemy, reveals a rebellious hatred toward God. From where does blasphemy originate according to Jesus in **Mark 7:20-23** (KJV; *slander* in other versions)?

Blasphemy may occur by defaming God's character, accusing Him of some evil or by not giving Him credit for His good works.

What was the punishment for blasphemy under the Mosaic Law, according to **Leviticus 24:15-16**?

2. Job's children, enjoying their father's wealth, entertained one another with extended celebrations and feasts. Afterward, Job interceded for them in case they had denied or forgotten God (Job 1:5). Read **Proverbs 30:7-9** and **Deuteronomy 8:10-19**. How might wealth have affected their devotion to the LORD?

Satan predicted that Job would curse God if he lost his wealth, family and health (Job 1:11; 2:5). Job's response to the losses, recorded in **Job 1:21a**, reflects his attitude toward wealth. What was his attitude?

How might wealth or poverty affect your devotion to the LORD?

3. Satan's prediction that Job would not only curse God, but that he would curse Him to His face, indicated an open and public renunciation of God. Rather than cursing God, what did Job do in **Job 1:21b**?

When Job blessed God's name, he went above and beyond honoring God. The Hebrew word for "name" is *shem* (#8034), which is a mark of individuality and implies a person's character and reputation. [4] To bless God's name is to review the excellencies of His Person, His Word and His works and to respond to them. Job was honoring all that God represents in His character and reputation with a desire for God's fame and honor to be magnified. Included in the definition of *barak* is the bending of the knee and kneeling down to bless. [5] In the context of Job 1:20-21, Job demonstrated with his actions the essence of *barak* by openly and publicly kneeling in submission to the LORD's dealings with him.

How might you magnify God's fame and honor?

How might you diminish God's fame and honor?

4. In Job 2:9, Mrs. Job urged Job to *"curse God and die."* Some commentaries are gracious to Mrs. Job by suggesting that she was so grieved by her husband's suffering, that she intended that he be relieved in whatever way possible. Based upon what you have learned about what it means to curse God, do you think that Mrs. Job's suggestion was any different from Satan's prediction and subsequent temptations for Job to curse God? Why or why not?

In his response to Mrs. Job, how did Job defend God's providence **(Job 2:10)**?

To summarize, what Job feared of his sons, what Satan hoped to elicit from Job and what Mrs. Job urged Job to do was to defame and attack the very character, providence and reputation of God. To do so would have been to distort His attributes, to make Him out to be less than He is, rather than to give God the full honor, praise and glory He is due.

5. Remembering that *barak* can mean to bless as well as to curse, we want to bless and to honor God's name. Job's act of blessing God was done openly and publicly and was published for later generations to read. Bless the name of the LORD today by reading and meditating upon Job 1:21 and Psalm 113:1-5. Then intentionally seek out someone to whom you may proclaim the following psalm of praise:

Praise the LORD!
Praise, O Servants of the LORD,
Praise the name of the LORD.
Blessed be the name of the LORD
From this time forth and forever.
From the rising of the sun to its setting
The name of the LORD is to be praised.
The LORD is high above all nations;
His glory is above the heavens.
Who is like the LORD our God,
Who is enthroned on high.

—Psalm 113:1-5

Day 2—Having Integrity

The LORD said to Satan, "Have you considered My servant Job? For there is no one like him on the earth, a blameless and upright man fearing God and turning away from evil. And he still holds fast his integrity."

—Job 2:3

Assignment: 1. Review Job 1 and 2.
2. Research words using Bible dictionaries.

In this lesson we will heed God's counsel to "consider My servant Job." We will explore what it meant in Job's day and what it means to us today to be blameless and upright. One commentary defined blamelessness in Job's day as the absence of certain sinful acts.

1. Look up the word *blameless/integrity* (#8535 and #8538) in a Bible dictionary. Write the definition.

Though the definitions include perfect, that does not mean sinless. There has been only one sinless man, the Lord Jesus Christ. The more appropriate definition for *blameless* and *perfect* is complete and entire, having integrity and without hypocrisy. It is the aspect of having no falsehood or hypocrisy that John Calvin addressed in one of his sermons on the character of Job. He stated that the opposite of blamelessness is to have a "double heart" or "heart and heart," meaning to serve God half-heartedly. The characteristic of blamelessness "is attributed to Job to show that he had a pure and simple affection . . . that he did not serve God only half, but he tried to give himself entirely to Him." [6]

What is a remedy for a "double heart," according to **Psalm 86:11?**

What are evidences in your own life that you are not half-hearted, but try to give yourself entirely to God?

2. Look up the definition for "upright" (#3477) in a Bible dictionary.

One of the clearest indicators that Job was upright and walked in a straight path was his intercession for his sons. **Job 1:5** is printed below. Circle the words that demonstrate Job's blamelessness (wholeheartedness) and uprightness (walking a straight, smooth and level path).

And it came about, when the days of feasting had completed their cycle, that Job would send and consecrate them, rising up early in the morning and offering burnt offerings according to the number of them all; for Job said, "Perhaps my sons have sinned and cursed God in their hearts." Thus Job did continually.

Do you want a straight path? Read **Proverbs 3:5-6** for the road map of a straight path. What is the road map?

3. Read **Job 2:3** and **Job 2:9**. What characteristic of Job did both God and Mrs. Job recognize was still intact, even during his excruciating illness?

In our day as well as in Job's day, blamelessness, uprightness and integrity are measured by outward actions. **Philippians 2:14-16** advises us of one way we can be blameless and innocent. Read the passage. What is that way?

Evaluate your own integrity, according to this passage. Would your family and friends agree with your self-evaluation? Would God?

Future lessons will explore what it means to grumble and complain. At that point, it will be important to remember that blameless does not mean sinless!

In all honesty, sincerity and singleness of purpose, Job maintained his wholehearted devotion to God. That is evidence of enduring faith.

As you know, we consider blessed those who have persevered. You have heard of Job's perseverance.
—James 5:11 NIV

Day 3—Fearing God

Job . . . a blameless and upright man fearing God.
—Job 2:3

Assignment: Read selected passages.

Yesterday you considered Job's integrity. God recognized Job for another excellence in character. Read **Job 1:8-9**. Of all of Job's qualities that God praised, which did Satan challenge?

Why did this bother Satan so much? In the Old Testament, people of faith were described as those who "fear the LORD." The fear of the LORD was the name for true devotion, which included confidence in

God, devotion to His Word, respect for His greatness and obedience to Him.[7] Therefore, it was Job's devotion to the LORD that Satan questioned and was intent upon destroying. Satan alleged that Job's devotion to God was strictly for the benefits he derived. Remove the benefits, Satan alleged, and Job's devotion would be removed as well. We have seen (Job 1:22; 2:10), however, that Satan underestimated Job's fear of the LORD. Twice!

1. Whether as a taunt or chastisement or an effort at encouragement, Eliphaz referred to Job's fear of the Lord. In **Job 4:6** what did he note about Job's fear of the Lord?

Thomas Watson, a Puritan pastor, explained that the fear of the Lord is a "fear springing from affection *(Hos. 3:5)*. A child fears to offend his father out of the tender affection he has for Him. . . . Faith and fear go hand in hand. When the soul looks at God's holiness, he fears. When he looks at God's promises, he believes. A godly man trembles, yet trusts."[8]

2. From the following verses, how did Job demonstrate his fear of the Lord in His devotion to God's Word?

Job 6:10

Job 23:12

3. "To man God said, 'Behold, the fear of the Lord, that is _____; and to depart from evil is _____.'" Job 28:28

Lord in Job 28:28 is *Adonay* (#136), which implies that the Lord as Owner has a claim upon man's obedience and service.[9] Early church father Anselm also took seriously the fear of the Lord, stating, "If sin were on one side and hell on the other, I would rather leap into hell than willingly offend my God."[10]

4. In **Job 37:23-24** Elihu identified several attributes of God that engender fear of Him. In speaking of God's transcendence, he described God as "the Almighty—we cannot find Him." That is, God is independent from man and His purposes are often hidden from man. According to these verses, what other attributes of God cause men to fear Him by respecting His greatness?

How did Job exhibit fear of the LORD by respecting His greatness?
Job 2:9-10; 9:4, 19

5. In his distress, Job lamented in Job 19:23, "Oh that my words were written! Oh, that they were inscribed in a book!"—And they were! You are reading them! God also has a book of remembrance that includes Job

and others who fear the LORD and who esteem His name:

> Then those who feared the LORD spoke to one another, and the LORD gave attention and heard it, and a book of remembrance was written before Him for those who fear the LORD and who esteem His name.

—Malachi 3:16

Do you fear the LORD and speak with other God-fearers about God's greatness? Do you esteem His name? Would Satan know you are a God-fearer? Would anyone know you fear the LORD? How would they know?

From what you have learned in today's lesson, how will you cultivate the fear of the LORD in your life?

Day 4—Turning From Temptation

> ***If I have walked with falsehood, And my foot has hastened after deceit, Let Him weigh me with accurate scales, and let God know my integrity.***
>
> *—Job 31:5-6*

Assignment: Read Job 31 and selected passages.

Job 1:1, 1:8 and 2:3 indicate that Job had developed a habit of turning away from evil. What kinds of evils were prevalent in Job's day? Ecclesiastes 1:9 says that there is nothing new under the sun. Men's hearts were the same then as now, and in Mark 7:21-23, Jesus warned us that sin proceeds from the heart.

1. Read **Job 31** and list some of the sins Job avoided.

   9-12

   16-18

   21-23

   24-25

   26-28

Job also claimed that he treated his workers fairly (13-15), clothed and fed those in his care (19-20, 31-32), did not rejoice over the misfortune of his enemies (29-30), had no hidden sins (33-34) and had not taken fruit of land that was not his (38-40). These verses demonstrate that long before Satan afflicted Job, Job had a lifestyle of turning away from evil. Therefore, when his wife urged him to "curse

God and die" (2:9), Job had a lifetime habit to rely upon to turn away from evil. His rebuke that she was speaking "as one of the foolish women speaks" (2:10) can be interpreted as, "Don't take on the thinking of those around you and of the world in which you live." What a wake-up call!

2. Today, as in Job's day, God's people are tempted to take on the thinking of the world around them. As with all habits, turning away from evil begins with a thought. Romans 12:2 challenges you "not to be conformed to this world, but be transformed by the renewing of your mind." When God gives a command, He also supplies the ability to carry out that command, as promised in 2 Peter 1:3: "seeing that His divine power has granted to us everything pertaining to life and godliness through the true knowledge of Him who called us by His own glory and excellence." Not only does God give the ability to carry out His commands; He instructs HOW to turn from evil.

You must first understand your vulnerability to sin and your utter dependence upon Christ to resist temptation. List the temptation/sin process outlined in **James 1:13-15.**

The phrase, "our own lusts", according to *The MacArthur Study Bible*, describes "the individual nature of lust—it is different for each person as a *result of inherited tendencies, environment, upbringing, and personal choices.* The Greek grammar also indicates that those 'desires' are the direct agent or cause of one's sinning." [11] (Emphasis added.) How vital it is to understand the influences that mold your desires, so that you will be aware of your own personal temptations!

Make a personal assessment by answering the questions below.

What particular sin do I habitually commit?

What temptation is especially enticing to me?

What generational sin has run in my family (drunkenness, physical/verbal abuse, etc.)?

What sinful relationship pattern have I developed since childhood?

What personal choices have I made that were sinful or led to sin?

3. Because of who we are in Christ, we are not enslaved to our past. Romans 6:22 assures us that we have been freed from sin and enslaved to God. We are now slaves to righteousness (Romans 6:19) and empowered by the Holy Spirit to resist temptation. God's commands are accompanied by truths that are freeing and life-changing. In theology, this is called the Indicative/Imperative motif. Read **1 Peter 1:13-19** printed below. This passage is an excellent example of the twin blessings of commands and truths that God gives us. Write a "C" in the blanks for the commands and a "T" for the life-changing truths. The first two

are identified for you.

__C__ Therefore, prepare your minds for action, keep sober in spirit, fix your hope completely

__T__ on the grace to be brought to you at the revelation of Jesus Christ.

_____ As obedient children, do not be conformed to the former lusts which were yours in your ignorance,

_____ but like the Holy One who called you,

_____ be holy yourselves also in all your behavior;

_____ because it is written, "YOU SHALL BE HOLY, FOR I AM HOLY."

_____ If you address as Father the One who impartially judges according to each one's work,

_____ conduct yourselves in fear during the time of your stay on earth;

_____ knowing that you were not redeemed with perishable things like silver or gold from your futile way of life inherited from your forefathers,

_____ but with precious blood, as of a lamb unblemished and spotless, the blood of Christ.

When confronted with any of temptations/ sins you identified in your personal assessment, on what life-changing truth from 1 Peter 1:13-19 can you focus to help you to obey God's commands?

It has been said that Martin Luther compared temptation to a bird flying about your head. His caution was that though the bird may fly, you do not have to let it land and build a nest in your hair. Yes, tempting thoughts will come. But believers do not need to give in to temptation. We have the resources of heaven itself to draw upon. According to **1 Corinthians 10:13**, what help does God the Father provide?

Nor do you battle temptation alone. In times of temptation it is comforting to know that Christ is interceding for you (Luke 22:31-32, Romans 8:34 and Hebrews 7:25). Along the way, tempting thoughts occur. The believer struggles against them, prays about them and asks for truth. The Lord often provides in His time and in His way a scripture, a teaching, a sermon, a book, a seminar, a phrase or sentence from another believer to correct the thought and to provide truth. His Holy Spirit strengthens and leads (Romans 8:13-14). The process cannot be formulated or ritualized. Success in battling temptation depends on walking closely with the Lord.

But what about when you've blown it, have succumbed to temptation and have sinned? Psalm 51:17 assures us that God does not despise a broken and contrite heart. Like Job in 42:6, repent, hate the sin and turn from it.

Has the Lord brought to mind any thought or action that you need to repent of, hate and turn from?

Your next assignment will further develop the biblical ways to turn from evil.

Day 5—Turning From Evil

I have made a covenant with my eyes.

—Job 31:1

Assignment: 1. Review Job 31.
               2. Read selected passages and answer questions.

Job indicated in 31:1 how he maintained purity. He made a covenant with his eyes that he would not lust after a woman. Such a covenant or promise was a premeditated decision to turn from evil. Puritan pastor John Owen observed, "Be killing sin or it will kill you." [12] Romans 8:13 states, "for if you are living according to the flesh, you must die; but if by the Spirit you are putting to death the deeds of the body, you will live." In the process of progressive sanctification the Christian battles sin, bears fruit, becomes holy and becomes more and more like Christ. Progressive sanctification begins at the moment of salvation, continues throughout the Christian's life on this earth and is completed on "the day of Christ Jesus" (Philippians 1:6). We must be aware that we will not be completely rid of sin in this life, but that we will be in a constant daily battle with sinful thoughts and sinful actions.

1. Job took the battle of sin so seriously that in Job 31 he called down serious consequences upon himself if he ever committed such sins. Similarly, Jesus Christ taught his followers "radical amputation" of sins. He was concerned with sinful thoughts as well as sinful deeds. Read **Matthew 5:28-30**. How seriously are His followers to deal with sins in their lives?

2. According to **2 Corinthians 10:3-5**, what are you to do with speculations, worries, daydreams, fantasies and other thoughts?

Identify any sinful thoughts in your life that you must "take captive to the obedience of Christ."
Instead of sinful thoughts, **Philippians 4:8** tells you to let your mind dwell on what things?

Practice choosing a godly thought that opposes the sinful thought. For example, if you are worried over finances, a godly replacement would be Philippians 4:19: "And my God shall supply all your needs according to His riches in glory in Christ

Jesus."

3. Turning away from evil also involves deliberate deeds. Read the following, known as the "put off-put on" passages and answer the questions below.

> . . . that you put off, concerning your former conduct, the old man which grows corrupt according to the deceitful lusts, and be renewed in the spirit of your mind, and that you put on the new man which was created according to God, in true righteousness and holiness.

> —Ephesians 4:22-24 NKJ

> Therefore consider the members of your earthly body as dead to immorality, impurity, passion, evil desire, and greed, which amounts to idolatry . . . But now you also, put them all aside: anger, wrath, malice, slander, and abusive speech from your mouth. Do not lie to one another, since you laid aside the old self with its evil practices, and have put on the new self who is being renewed to a true knowledge according to the image of the One who created him—a renewal in which there is no distinction between Greek and Jew, circumcised and uncircumcised, barbarian, Scythian, slave and freeman, but Christ is all, and in all. So, as those who have been chosen of God, holy and beloved, put on a heart of compassion, kindness, humility, gentleness and patience; bearing with one another, and forgiving each other, whoever has a complaint against anyone; just as the Lord forgave you, so also should you. Beyond all these things put on love, which is the perfect bond of unity. Let the peace of Christ rule in your hearts, to which indeed you were called in one body; and be thankful.

> —Colossians 3:5, 8-15 NASU

Circle what you are to "put off."

Underline what you are to "put on."

Now write the qualities that, with the help of God's Spirit, you will add to your life to replace the sins you now reject.

Knowing God's Word is crucial to the battle for your mind. Meditating on and memorizing scripture will help you to let go of old sinful thoughts and habits. Recall from the Job survey what value Job placed on the words of God's mouth (Job 23:11-12).

Choose a scripture to commit to memory from those you have read today. Write it below.

OPTIONAL

To reinforce your new thought pattern, you may write your own Job 31 on the form at the end of this day's lesson. On it, identify your current temptation and the scripture you have chosen to counter it. Thank God for His strength and provision for you to turn from sin. Thank Him that your sins have been forgiven through Jesus Christ.

My Personal Job 31

I have made a covenant with my (hands, heart, eyes, ears, or other) _____

How then could I (name your current temptation) _____

To counter temptation I will meditate on _____

Have I covered my transgressions like Adam, By hiding my iniquity in my bosom?

—Job 31:33

Lord, please bring to light any unconfessed sin.

If I have _____

Let Him weigh me with accurate scales, and let God know my integrity.

If my step_____

If my heart_____

If I have_____

If I have_____

A broken and contrite heart, O God, You will not despise.

—Psalm 51:17

In accordance with Ephesians 4:22-32 and Colossians 3:5-15,

I put off

And I put on

Thank You, Lord, that my righteousness is not my own, but that which comes by faith in Christ Jesus, the righteousness which comes from God based on faith that You give to me. Thank You for the example of Job, who pleased You by turning from evil.

—Prayer adapted from Philippians 3:9

Figure 5.1 My Personal Job 31

REFLECTIONS ON LESSON 5

Truths I have learned that deepen my relationship with the Lord

Day 1

What was Satan's goal in tempting Job to curse God?

Looking back over your actions and thoughts this week, did you in any way dishonor God?

How did you magnify God's honor?

Day 2

How has your study of Job's integrity challenged you?

Explain the difference between blameless and sinless.

Day 3

Why did Job's fear of God bother Satan so much?

How does fear of the LORD work as a deterrent to sin in your life?

Day 4

Because God instructs us not to be conformed to the thinking of this world, what are some ways you can renew your mind?

Day 5

What is one step you can take now to develop a lifestyle of turning away from evil?

Notes

1. *Vine's Complete Expository Dictionary of Old and New Testament Words* (Nashville: Nelson, 1985. Copyright 1985 by Thomas Nelson), 18.

2. *Matthew Henry's Commentary of the Whole Bible* (Peabody, MA: Hendrickson, 1991. Copyright 1991 by Hendrickson), 656.

3. Jerome H. Smith, *The New Treasury of Scripture Knowledge* (Nashville: Nelson, 1992. Copyright 1962 by Jerome H. Smith), 550.

4. *Strong's Complete Word Study Concordance* (Chattanooga, TN: AMG, 2004. Copyright 2004 by AMG), 1988.

5. *Vine's*, 18.

6. John Calvin, *Sermons from Job* (Grand Rapids: Baker, 1979. Copyright 1952 by Wm. B. Eerdmans), 10.

7. Spiros Zodhiates, *Hebrew-Greek Key Word Study Bible* (Chattanooga, TN: AMG, 1990. Copyright 1984 and 1990 by AMG), 1733.

8. Thomas Watson, *The Godly Man's Picture*, (Originally published in 1666; Carlisle, PA: Banner of Truth Trust, 2003), 178.

9. *Strong's*, 1805.

10. Watson, 178.

11. John MacArthur, *The MacArthur Study Bible* (Nashville: Word, 1997. Copyright 1997 by Word), 1927.

12. John Owen, *Triumph Over Temptation* (Colorado Springs: Cook, 2005. Copyright 2005 by James M. Houston), 202.

LESSON 6 GOD'S SOVEREIGNTY

Day 1—God's All-sufficiency

Can you discover the depths of God? Can you discover the limits of the Almighty [all-sufficient One]?

—Job 11:7

Assignment: 1. Read selected passages.
2. Locate figures 0.2 through 0.4 in the Introduction and review the *Attributes of God* charts. You will use them for the rest of the study.
3. Record scriptures meaningful to you from this lesson in figure 0.2, the *Attributes of God—All-sufficiency* chart.

We learn much about God's attributes from the book of Job. God's attributes are truths about Himself that He has chosen to reveal to us through His Word. Attributes describe His divine character, who He is. Beginning today and throughout the remainder of the study, you will encounter God as He has revealed Himself in the book of Job. You will see His character in the following attributes:

All-sufficiency
Sovereignty, omnipotence and providence
Righteousness and justice
Incomprehensibility and transcendence
Wisdom and omniscience
Lovingkindness

1. Have you heard some say that God must have created people because He was lonely, bored or incomplete? Eliphaz, Job and God Himself weigh in on those ideas.

Read the following statements by Eliphaz; then write his conclusion.

4:18

15:15-16

22:2-3

Conclusion:

What did Job say about God's all-sufficiency in **21:22**?

What did God Himself say about His all-sufficiency in **41:11**?

2. The book of Job contrasts some aspects of man's insufficiency with God's all-sufficiency. Identify those aspects in the verses noted in table 6.1.

3. Astonishingly, even though God doesn't need us, He desires a relationship with His creatures. Study the definition featured in figure 6.1 of God's all-sufficiency. Job described such a relationship in **14:15**. What is the basis of that relationship?

GOD'S ALL-SUFFICIENCY

God is self-sufficient and does not need man.

God is unaffected by man's wickedness or man's righteousness, yet He cares for man.

God gains nothing from us,

yet He desires a relationship with us

and has provided the means for that relationship.

Figure 6.1. Definition of God's all-sufficiency

Table 6.1 Contrast of man's insufficiency and God's all-sufficiency

CONTRAST OF MAN'S INSUFFICIENCY AND GOD'S ALL-SUFFICIENCY	
Man's Insufficiency	**God's All-sufficiency**
7:1	23:13-14
	42:2
7:9	36:26
14:1-2	
14:4	11:7-9
25:4-6	25:2
40:4	
31:14	21:22

God in His all-sufficiency has provided a way that lowly man might be right with Him and give Him glory. In Lesson 10 you will study God's provision for man to have a relationship with Him.

Now, turn to figure 0.2, the *Attributes of God—All-sufficiency* chart you reviewed at the beginning of this lesson. Record your favorite verse from today's assignment. From now to the end of the JOB study, take advantage of the opportunity to compile your favorite verses.

Day 2—God's Sovereignty and Omnipotence

The LORD gave and the LORD has taken away.

—Job 1:21

Assignment: 1. Read selected scriptures.
2. Record in figure 0.2, the *Attributes of God—-Sovereignty* chart.

Today and tomorrow you will be introduced to three of God's attributes: sovereignty, omnipotence and providence. You will learn to recognize them as you further study Job from a God-centered perspective. *God's sovereignty* means that He rules over all. There is nothing outside of His control. In full freedom God carries out His plans and purposes. He has full power to do so. His *omnipotence*, or His ability to rule and to carry out His plans and purposes, cannot be thwarted. God's *providence* is His active involvement in governing and providing for His creation. On a personal level, providence is the outworking of God's will in a person's life. Study the definitions of God's sovereignty, omnipotence and providence in figure 6.2.

GOD'S SOVEREIGNTY, OMNIPOTENCE AND PROVIDENCE
God's sovereignty means that God rules over all and controls all things.
God's omnipotence is His ability to rule.
God's providence is His active involvement in governing and sustaining
His creation for His own plans and purposes.

Figure 6.2. Definitions of God's sovereignty, omnipotence and providence

1. Acknowledging God's sovereignty is foundational to the study of the book of Job. How did God assert His authority at the beginning?

1:12, 2:6

God's rule was never disputed in any of the debates of chapters 4 through 37. In fact, God's sovereignty was proclaimed eloquently by Job and Elihu. Read the passages below and summarize what you learn about God's sovereignty.

12:9-10

34:13-15

How did God strongly assert His authority to Job at the end of the book?

41:11

How did Job acknowledge in **1:21** and **2:10** God's rule over his life?

Is there any area of your life or any circumstance where you have been resisting God's sovereignty, His rule? Are you ready to agree with Job to bless the name of the LORD at all times?

2. Consider God's omnipotence. Displays of God's power elicit questions reflecting a sense of being overwhelmed by its awfulness and awesomeness. Finish the following questions raised in Job.

9:4 Wise in heart and mighty in strength,

9:12 Were He to snatch away,

9:12 Who could say to Him,

9:19 If it is a matter of power, behold, He is the strong one! And if it is a matter of justice,

11:10 If He passes by or shuts up, or calls an assembly,

23:13 He is unique

36:22 God is exalted in His power;

God crowned his final speech with vivid descriptions of Behemoth and Leviathan, the fiercest of all of His creatures, to give Job an indication of His divine power. What comparison with Leviathan did He make in **41:10**?

What was Job's response in **42:2** to God's graphic lesson about His omnipotence?

What is your response to God's omnipotence?

How does God's power comfort you?

How does it frighten you?

Praise God that He is not a capricious God who exerts His power by senseless whim. Rather, we serve a God who exercises His power for His purposeful design, which you will study about in tomorrow's lesson.

Day 3—God's Providence

For He performs what is appointed for me, And many such decrees are with Him.

—Job 23:14

Assignment: 1. Read selected scriptures.
2. Record in figure 0.2, the *Attributes of God—Sovereignty Chart.*

The thought of the *providence* of God, that He orchestrates every aspect of your life, is very comforting until it runs counter to your own plans and purposes. In Job 23:14, Job acknowledged that God "performs what is appointed for me, and many such decrees are with Him." Like Job, some would agree that God rules over all, but they would question God's purposes and would seek to interpret His dealings with them. Ephesians 1:11 assures us that God "works all things after the counsel of His will." He has made known what some have called His *revealed or moral will* in the Bible, especially in the 10 Commandments and the New Testament.[1] Although you can be sure that God's plan is perfect, all-inclusive and for your ultimate good, most often it is hidden from you. God's *hidden will* is known only in retrospect, if at all. John J. Murray has noted regarding God's secret will, "God hides it from me until it happens. I discover it day by day as the plan unfolds." [2]

1. How does **Deuteronomy 29:29** guide us to a proper perspective of God's hidden and revealed will?

2. What was revealed to the reader about God's secret will for Job in **1:8-12** and **2:3-6**?

Though Job remained ignorant about God's purpose in appointing suffering for him, he still acknowledged God's providence, as you read in Job 23:14.

Identify a situation for which you want answers. Is the answer you are seeking already spelled out in God's Word? And you are dissatisfied with it? Or is the answer a secret thing of God's that you need to leave alone?

3. In His providence God governs and sustains creation and man for His own purposes. He created all things and preserves the course of nature, providing food and residences for His creatures and an order to their lives utilizing water and dry land, day and night, light and dark, the variety of seasons, weather and all other wonders of creation. God's providence is absolutely wise and mysterious. List several of *"the fringes of His ways"* according to **Job 26:5-14**.

4. God governs the affairs of men, from the giving of life and length of days, to his place among other men. He raises up leaders and brings them down. What does **Job 12:13-25** reveal about God's involvement in the affairs of:

Man (**14**)

Misleader and misled (**16**)

Kings (**18**)

Priests (**19**)

Elders (**20**)

Nobles (**21**)

Global leaders (**24-25**)

The *Westminster Confession of Faith of 1646* (Chapter 5 Section 1) defines providence in the following way:

God, the great Creator of all things, doth uphold, direct, dispose and govern all creatures, actions, and things, from the greatest even to the least, by his most wise and holy providence, according to his infallible foreknowledge, and the free and immutable counsel of his own will, to the praise of the glory of his wisdom, power, justice, goodness, and mercy.[3]

Notice the above definition of providence includes many attributes of God, reminding us that God will not act in any way that is contrary to His character. Job, recognizing the fullness of God's attributes, exclaimed, "With Him are wisdom and might; to Him belong counsel and understanding" (Job 12:13).

5. Read the verse below and circle the two attributes of God that Job understood to work together for his protection.

You gave me life and showed me kindness and in your providence watched over my spirit.
—Job 10:12 NIV

How does your understanding of God's providence in the earthly realm affect your view of God?

Praise God for the amazing completeness and sufficiency of His character.

Day 4—God's Sovereignty Over the Heavenly Realm

Now there was a day when the sons of God came to present themselves before the LORD, and Satan also came among them.

—Job 1:6

Assignment: 1. Review Job 1 and 2 and read selected passages.
2. Record in figure 0.2, the *Attributes of God—Sovereignty* chart.

In Job 1:6-12 and 2:1-6, we see God at work in the heavenly realm. Some commentators refer to the two scenes as divine assemblies or heavenly councils. In the historic Near East, the idea of a council or a meeting of the gods was commonly accepted. The gods would meet to discuss strategy and important matters and to lay plans for the future. The tone of the councils was often combative and unpleasant as the gods jockeyed for power and position.[4] In Job we have one of the few glimpses of God's heavenly rule.

1. In the Job passages, who is presiding over the council?

1:6, 2:1

What indicates who is presiding?

1:6, 2:1

2. For other Old Testament glimpses of heavenly councils, read the following verses and summarize the meetings.

1 Kings 22:19-23

Isaiah 6:1-8

Jeremiah 23:18, 22

Psalm 89:5-7

3. For a bold look at the Sovereign ruler over the council, read and write out **Psalm 115:3**.

. . . because God is God, He does as He pleases, only as He pleases, always as He pleases; that His great concern is the accomplishment of His own pleasure and the promotion of His own glory; that He is the Supreme Being, and therefore Sovereign of the universe.[5]

4. Look up and record the verses in table 6.2 that give further insight into how God is sovereign over the heavenly realm.

Table 6.2 God's sovereignty in the heavenly realm

GOD'S SOVEREIGNTY IN THE HEAVENLY REALM		
Reference	Over what is God sovereign?	How does He show power and authority?
1 Chronicles 21:15, 27		
Psalm 91:11		
Daniel 6:22		
Matthew 13:41		
Matthew 24:31		
Acts 12:11		

5. Using scriptures from your lesson today, list in figure 0.2, the *Attributes of God–Sovereignty* chart the references about God's sovereignty that are most meaningful to you.

Today our focus has been on God's sovereignty in the heavenly realm. Tomorrow you will see with confidence that God is also Sovereign Ruler over evil Satan, whose main purpose is to rain deception and destruction on man.

How does your understanding of God's sovereignty in the heavenly realm affect your view of God?

Day 5—God's Sovereignty Over Satan

So the LORD said to Satan, 'Behold, he is in your power, only spare his life.'
—Job 2:6

Assignment: 1. Review Job 1 and 2.
2. Use a Bible expository dictionary. Refer to *A Word About Word Studies* located in the Introduction.
3. Record in figure 0.2, the *Attributes of God—Sovereignty* chart.

The most complete picture of Satan in the Old Testament appears in the first two chapters of Job, according to one commentator. Some translations place a definite article before the name Satan, rendering the reading "the Satan," which emphasizes that he is not just <u>an</u> adversary but <u>THE</u> Adversary.[6] One minor viewpoint is that the evil character in Job 1 and 2 is not Satan of the New Testament but one of the "sons of God" (Job 1:6), who challenges the Lord. He is a member of the heavenly council, yet must work within God's sovereign boundaries.[7]

But most scholars hold that Satan of the Old Testament and Satan of the New Testament are one and the same (Revelation 12:7-9). William Henry Green points out the harmony between Satan's character in Job and his character throughout the rest of scripture:

> He is not a mere spy, traversing the earth and intent upon ferreting out all that he can discover. He is the old spirit of malice and wickedness, aiming to pervert men from the right ways of the LORD, and to destroy all goodness as far as it is in his power.
>
> And there is a profound meaning in his appearing here among the sons of God before the LORD. It is designed to express his subordination and subjection to divine control.[8]

1. Look up the word Satan in the Old Testament section of a Bible dictionary. What does the title Satan mean (#7854)?

How many times is it used in the Old Testament?

Satan has many other titles and descriptive names—none of them complimentary—in the   Word of God. He is called accuser of the brethren, serpent, ruler of the demons, the devil, murderer, liar, father of lies and ruler and god of the world.

2. God is infinite but Satan is finite. Satan is the accepted head of the fallen angels about whom we read in 2 Peter 2:4 and Jude 6. He is a created being, subservient to Creator God. Though he rebelled against God and roams to and fro (Job 1:7), seeking to devour whom he can (1 Peter 5:8), his days are numbered

(Revelation 12:12). He is not omnipotent or omniscient. According to Irving L. Jensen, "Satan is not omnipresent but he can work simultaneously in the hearts of people all over the world through his subordinates—evil angels and evil spirits." [9] Satan does not know your thoughts; God alone knows them (Psalm 139:2-4). Below, some of his wicked activities are contrasted with God's overriding authority.

- He tempted Adam and Eve to sin (Genesis 3:1-5).

  Yet God is sovereign. What curse and fatal blow did God declare upon Satan, the serpent in **Genesis 3:14-15**?

- He temporarily usurps authority over the earth (Luke 4:6).

  Yet God is sovereign. What victory did Jesus claim in **Matthew 28:18** because of His crucifixion and resurrection?

- He dominates and captivates sinners (Acts 26:18).

  Yet God is sovereign. **Colossians 1:13** states that God the Father has delivered us from the _____ of _____ and has _____ us to the _____ of His beloved _____.

- He snatches away the seed of the gospel (Matthew 13:19).

  Yet God is sovereign. Read **John 10:28-29** and write below how the *good* seed of the gospel is made snatch-proof.

- He slanders the saints (Job 1:9-11).

  Yet God is sovereign. What will God do to the accuser of the brethren, according to **Revelation 12:10**?

- He wrestles "in the heavenly places" against the saints (Ephesians 6:12).

  Yet God is sovereign. The book of Job affirms that "Dominion and awe belong to Him [God]" (Job 25:2).

Read the remainder of that verse to learn where God establishes order and imposes His peace.

  Which activity of Satan listed above causes you alarm?

God in His great mercy to believers shows them how to do battle with Satan. A Christian is to put on the full armor of God (Ephesians 6:10-18) because he can expect to be at war throughout his life. The belt of truth enables him to continually think on God's promises and on what is real (truth), not on what is imagined and false. Wearing the breastplate of righteousness, the Christian depends upon Jesus' work on the cross to pay for his sins and to make him worthy to stand in the presence of Holy God. The gospel shoes of peace present the message of peace with God through Jesus Christ wherever he goes. The shield of faith is confident obedience to the Word of God regardless of circumstances or consequences. It shelters him from temptations and barbed accusations of the evil one. The helmet of salvation is assurance that he belongs to God and God belongs to him. The believer is to pray in the Spirit at all times. Notice that the full armor of God is defensive against Satan except for the sword of the Spirit, the believer's only offensive weapon. That sword is the Word of God, and to brandish it as a skilled fencer, the Christian must know and appreciate the eternal power of God's Word.

Take time to meditate on the scriptures referenced and record in figure 0.2, the Attributes of God—Sovereignty *chart. Rest assured of your victory in Jesus.*

3. In revealing Satan's activity through the book of Job, God surely does not intend for us to become preoccupied with Satan. Rather, God is alerting us to the worldly powers that are stronger than we are, yet are miniscule in comparison to His own powers. With no strength of our own, the Christian must depend upon God's empowerment to battle Satan. As you close your study for today, spend time in prayer thanking God for your salvation, for being your "Mighty Fortress" in the daily temptations and rigors of life here on this earth. The words of Martin Luther's great hymn of the same title follow.

What does Luther affirm about Satan and his power? _____

_____

What does he conclude about our ability to resist and battle Satan? _____

_____

To what does he direct us to win this battle? _____

_____

How can this be practically applied in your life? _____

_____

A Mighty Fortress

A Mighty fortress is our God; A bulwark never failing;
Our helper He, amid the flood of mortal ills prevailing;
For still our ancient foe doth seek to work us woe;
 His craft and pow'r are great,
And, armed with cruel hate,
On earth is not his equal.

Did we in our own strength confide, our striving would be losing;
Were not the right Man on our side, the Man of God's own choosing;
Dost ask who that may be? Christ Jesus, it is He;
Lord Sabaoth, His name,
From age to age the same,
And He must win the battle.

And tho' this world with devils filled, should threaten to undo us;
We will not fear, for God hath willed His truth to triumph thro' us:
The Prince of Darkness grim, we tremble not for him;
His rage we can endure,
For lo, his doom is sure,
One little word shall fell him.

That word above all earthly pow'rs, no thanks to them, abideth;
The Spirit and the gifts are ours thro' Him who with us sideth:
 Let goods and kindred go, This mortal life also;
The body they may kill:
God's truth abideth still,
His kingdom is forever. [10]

Martin Luther

REFLECTIONS ON LESSON 6

Truths I have learned that deepen my relationship with the Lord

Day 1

In what way(s) does the view of God's all-sufficiency presented in the book of Job differ from the modern view in our culture?

Day 2

Give an example of God's sovereignty in your life.

Give an example of God's omnipotence in your life.

Day 3

Review Question 4. What example of God's providence from Job 12:13-25 have you witnessed?

Describe the circumstances from God's perspective, finishing the sentence, "In God's providence . . ."

Give an example of God's providence in your life.

Day 4

Name some of God's activities in the heavenly realm.

According to A.W. Pink's quote, what is God's concern for His activity in the heavenly realm?

Day 5

Are there any of Satan's wicked activities listed in question 2 which you are observing around you now? Explain.

According to "A Mighty Fortress" and Ephesians 6:10-18, what resources has God provided for you to combat Satan's activity?

Notes

1. Wayne Grudem, *Systematic Theology* (Leicester, England: Inter-Varsity, 1994. Copyright 1994 by Wayne Grudem), 332.

2. John J. Murray, *Beyond a Frowning Providence* (Carlisle, PA: Banner of Truth Trust, 1990. Copyright 1990 by Banner of Truth Trust), 10.

3. *Westminster Confession of Faith of 1646* Chapter 5 Section 1. http://www.reformed.org/documents/wcf_with_proofs/ch_V.html (accessed 8/22/2010).

4. Leland Ryken, James C. Willhoit and Tremper Longman III, ed., *Dictionary of Biblical Imagery* (Downers Grove, IL: Intervarsity Press, 1998. Copyright 1998 by Inter-Varsity Christian Fellowship/USA), 760.

5. Arthur W. Pink, *The Sovereignty of God* (Grand Rapids: Baker, 2006. Copyright 1930 by I. C. Herendeen), 17.

6. David D. Garland, *JOB, A Study Guide* (Grand Rapids: Zondervan, 1971. Copyright 1971 by Zondervan), 20.

7. William Henry Green, *Conflict and Triumph* (Carlisle, PA: Banner of Truth Trust, 1999. Copyright 1999 by Banner of Truth Trust), 20.

8. Green, 21.

9. Irving L. Jensen, *JOB* (Chicago: Moody, 1975. Copyright 1975 by Moody Bible Institute of Chicago), 27.

10. Martin Luther, Public Domain.

LESSON 7 GOD'S CHARACTER

Day 1—God's Wisdom and Omniscience

Consider...the wonders of One perfect in knowledge.

—Job 37:14, 16

Assignment: 1. Read selected passages.
2. Record scriptures meaningful to you from this lesson in figure 0.3, the *Attributes of God—Wisdom and Omniscience* chart.

God is the Source of true wisdom and knowledge (Job 28:23-27). Elihu, who claimed to get his knowledge from "afar" (Job 36:3), possibly referring to heaven, directed Job to consider "the wonders of Him who is perfect in knowledge" (Job 37:16). God is perfect in knowledge because He knows everything; nothing is hidden from Him. In wisdom, God knows how to bring about His plan; He knows and does what is best, what accomplishes His purposes. Study the definitions of God's wisdom and omniscience in figure 7.1.

> **GOD'S WISDOM and OMNISCIENCE**
> God knows how to bring about His plan.
> God knows and does what is best.
> God is omniscient or all-knowing, perfect in knowledge.
> Nothing is hidden from God.

Figure 7.1. Definitions of God's wisdom and omniscience

1. Our omniscient God knows everything about all things and all people. How is God's knowledge of all

things described?

12:22

26:6, 9

The relational aspect of God's knowledge in the book of Job refers to God's knowledge of man's ways. What does God know without investigating, according to Zophar in **11:11**?

Based on **34:21**, what do God's eyes see?

What was Job's attitude toward God's intimate knowledge of his ways?

23:10

31:4-6

These two qualities of God's knowledge, that He has all the facts and that He knows men intimately, make Him the perfect Judge. Job 21:22 concludes: "Can anyone teach God knowledge, In that He judges those on high?"

2. God's wisdom is described poetically in the book of Job. Match the following references to the corresponding descriptions.

God's Wisdom:

9:4	**purposefully numbers the clouds**
11:6	**is strong and sound**
12:13	**is vast and indisputable**
12:16	**is secret and hidden**
38:37	**includes counsel and understanding**

3. Job believed that only God's wisdom could explain his suffering (28:24). Applying the definitions of God's knowledge and wisdom that you have learned in this lesson, explain Job's suffering from a God-centered perspective.

What situation in your life might be explained by applying the definitions of God's knowledge and wisdom?

What detail of God's knowledge and wisdom is especially meaningful to you right now?

Why?

Day 2—God's Incomprehensibility, Transcendence and Lovingkindness

[God] Who does great and unsearchable things, Wonders without number.

—Job 5:9

Assignment: 1. Read selected passages.
2. Record scriptures meaningful to you from this lesson in figure 0.4, the *Attributes of God— Incomprehensibility and Lovingkindness* charts.

Job's and his friends' attempts to use human reasoning to explain his suffering had limits. For them and for us, human probing of God's role in human suffering always falls short! Ultimately, our all-sufficient God is fully capable of defending His own character and actions, as He demonstrated at the end of the book of Job. Questions not answered to human satisfaction have answers known only to God which are hidden for His own purposes (Deuteronomy 29:29). Our human limitations magnify God's incomprehensibility and transcendence, defined in figure 7.2.

GOD'S INCOMPREHENSIBILITY and TRANSCENDENCE
God is incomprehensible so that we are not able to fully understand
His nature, character and ways.
This is also called the inscrutability of God.
God is transcendent.
He is all-sufficient, set apart from and beyond His creation.

Figure 7.2. Definitions of God's incomprehensibility and transcendence

1. The incomprehensibility and inscrutability of God mean that He is incapable of being searched out and understood, as His ways are mysterious. How do the following verses in Job reaffirm the the hiddenness of God?

    5:8-9

    11:7-9

    36:26

    37:5

    37:22-23

2. How do the following verses, also from Job, describe God as transcendent, beyond His creation?

    22:12

    35:5-7

God's incomprehensibility and transcendence mean that we cannot find Him without His help. Yet we are told in Job 22:21 (NKJV) to "acquaint yourself with Him and be at peace."

3. Because we can know God only by what He reveals about Himself, He condescends and   stoops down from His lofty heavens to make Himself known to us and to involve Himself intimately in our lives. God's involvement in creation is called His immanence, His nearness.   How are God's transcendence and immanence combined in **Isaiah 57:15**?

 How did the LORD condescend or stoop down to reveal Himself to Job in **chapters 38 through 41**, especially **38:1** and **40:6?**

4. Read **Job 7:17-18**. What was Job's assessment of God's involvement with man, especially with himself?

Though Job expressed frustration over God's scrutiny of him, he nonetheless identified God's concern for humans, literally, "that You should set Your heart on him [humans]." Psalm 8:4 similarly expresses, "What is man, that You take thought of him? And the son of man that you care for him?"

    The word "lovingkindness" is rarely used in the book of Job. In **Job 10:12**, what did Job say about God's lovingkindness?

    What did Elihu suggest about God's lovingkindness in **37:13?**

Both references in Job 10:12 and 37:13 employ the same Hebrew word *chesed* (#2617), which is translated as "lovingkindness," "mercy," "favor" or "grace." The *Key Word Study Bible* designates *chesed* as "one of the most important words" in the Hebrew Old Testament because it combines God's love with His mercy.[1] The New Testament also confirms God's lovingkindness: "the outcome of the Lord's dealings [with Job], [demonstrates] that the Lord is full of compassion and is merciful" (James 5:11).

5. **Psalm 113**, especially **verses 5 and 6**, is a praise of God's majesty and condescension. According to that psalm, what does God do to "behold the things that are in heaven and in the earth?"

How did Jesus describe God's condescending watch care over us in **Matthew 6:25-30?**

6. In God's ultimate revelation of Himself to people, He condescended from His heavenly throne to come to earth in human flesh to demonstrate His loving concern for those whom He set His heart upon for salvation. What do the following scriptures reveal about God's condescension to people through Jesus Christ?

    John 1:14

Hebrews 1:3

Philippians 2:5-11

We now have a working definition of God's lovingkindness, featured in figure 7.3.

GOD'S LOVINGKINDNESS
God is concerned for His creation, granting and preserving life.
The Lord is full of compassion and is merciful.

Figure 7.3. Definition of God's lovingkindness

God's attributes of sovereignty, omnipotence, incomprehensibility and transcendence may make Him seem distant from us. His providence, omniscience and lovingkindness demonstrate His presence with us, His nearness to us and His involvement with us. He is incomprehensible, yet His is also intimate with us. Though we, like Job and his friends, cannot understand God's ways, we must trust in His lovingkindness.

Praise God for His condescension in stooping down to make Himself known to you through Jesus Christ. Trust Him for His love.

Day 3—God's Righteousness

Does God pervert justice? Or does the Almighty pervert what is right?
—Job 8:3

Assignment: 1. Read selected passages.
2. Record in figure 0.3, the *Attributes of God—Justice* chart.

Job was building his case against God. His friends had already contrived a case against Job and declared him guilty. Both cases required a just Judge. Who would that be? As Job defended himself, he crossed a line. 1. Whether he liked it or not, Job had to weigh in on a heavy theological question: Is God just? Read **Job 9:20-23** and **Job 19:6-7** to find out what Job deduced about God's justice in order to maintain his own innocence.

Though I am _____ my mouth will condemn me. Though I am _____, He will declare me _____ (9:20). I am _____ (9:21) . . . 'He _____ the guiltless and the wicked' (9:22). . . . He _____ the despair of the innocent (9:23). . . . Know then that God has _____ me And has closed His net around me (19:6). . . . but there is no _____ (19:7).

This was a very pivotal position for Job in his suffering. He had now called God's justice into question. He had lost confidence in the justice of this God whom he knew to be wise, powerful and sovereign, a formidable foe no one would wisely challenge (9:4), but Job did.

2. Much of the book's dialogue is a defense of God's justice, culminating in a defense from God Himself. How do the following scriptures in Job uphold God's righteousness and justice?

8:3

21:22

34:19

36:3

37:23

The book of Job teaches that God's justice is undeviating, impartial and abundant. God's justice and righteousness have the same Hebrew root and are so closely linked that some theologians place them in the same category; they are translated interchangeably. Thus, our definitions of God's justice and righteousness, featured in figure 7.4, are combined as well.

> **GOD'S JUSTICE AND RIGHTEOUSNESS**
> God is always just and right in all He does.
> His justice is undeviating and abundant.
> God is the righteous, impartial Judge.
> God is jealous for His name.

Figure 7.4 Definitions of God's justice and righteousness

3. Justice is not only what God does, but it is also who He is, permeating His name, His reputation and His character. John Piper defines God's righteousness as "his unwavering commitment always to uphold and display the infinite value of his glory and his name."[2] What was the focus of God's rebuke of Job in **40:8**?

How has this study on God's righteousness helped you to understand the seriousness of questioning or discrediting God's justice?

How will you avoid questioning or discrediting God's justice in the future?

Remember to transfer some of your favorite scriptures from today's lesson to figure 0.3, the *Attributes of God – Justice/Righteousness* chart.

Day 4—God's Justice: Court Scene

Behold now, I have prepared my case.

—Job 13:18

Assignment: 1. Read **Job 31** as background for the trial.
2. Read selected passages from the book of Job and answer the questions.

Reading Job 31 can make an imaginative fellow reach for pen and paper. What passionate characters he could control! What vivid footage he could capture and spin electronically into your living room! What a subject! Justice meted out and not meted out in a fantastic courtroom scene presided over by an apparently absent Judge! Three guys acting as prosecutors, witnesses and jury! One man—plaintiff and defendant—delivering a great oath of innocence.

Perhaps you are an attorney or judge or have served on a jury. Or maybe you have been a defendant or a plaintiff in a court of law. In the land of Uz, Job, too, was familiar with the legal jargon and system of his day. Part of his reputation as "the greatest of all the men of the east" (Job 1:3) was based on his position of authority as a wise man who sat at the city gate (probably in the inner court), hearing cases and dispensing justice. Losing this honorable position and suffering the resulting mockery caused Job great anguish, as you have learned.

Even more terrible than his loss of authority was God's silence toward him. While Job pondered and protested God's silence and blamed Him for his suffering, he formed an idea to satisfy his longing for God's answers and justice. Job would take God to court; he would bring a lawsuit against God!

Scholars have sketchy information about the court systems of the Near East because laws varied from land to land. They do know that the laws of ancient cities always demanded a statement of prosecution and a statement of the defendant in rebuttal. The Bible is rich in detail about God's laws for the Israelites, but Job and his friends were not Israelites. Scholars caution the modern reader to not impose our modern concepts of law on Job and his claims against God, although for this study we will use several legal terms that are familiar.[3]

1. First, take a look at Job's thinking as he built his case against God. In his 'pre-trial' thoughts, what did Job lament?

9:32

What did he decide to do anyway?

10:1-2

In what manner did Job speak to the Almighty?

13:15 and 23:4

2. What are some of the complaints against God that Job included in his indictment?

9:20, 28

9:24

10:7

3. Job believed that his charges and complaints against God were true. He went as far as predicting the verdict at trial's end. What outcome was he confidently expecting?

13:18

23:5-7

In 25 words or less summarize Job's case against God.

Although you may not have considered your critical thoughts in terms of "taking Him to court," have you complained about God to Him? What were the circumstances? What was the outcome? (In Lesson 9, you will learn the difference between complaining <u>to</u> God and complaining <u>about</u> God.)

Day 5—God's Justice: Job's Oath of Innocence

If I have walked with falsehood And my foot has hastened after deceit, Let Him weigh me with accurate scales, And let God know my integrity.

—Job 31:5-6

Assignment: Review Job 31.

Chapter 31 of the book of Job is known as Job's great oath of innocence. Carefully review it and watch for this pattern: Job lists a specific sin and then spells out a consequence or judgment for that sin. Those dire consequences were the equivalent of curses in ancient Near East thinking.

Was Job admitting that he was guilty of those sins and then calling down curses on himself? No, Job had already claimed for himself a not-guilty verdict in his court case against God. Instead, by calling down curses on himself if he were guilty of any of the specific sins, he risked undergoing more suffering. But so certain was he of his integrity, he was willing to take that chance.

Job's action toward himself was significant, according to Robert L. Alden:

> Curses were taken very seriously by ancient Near Eastern people. Words, spoken or written, had real power, and to call down curses on oneself was a grave and daring thing to do....By this means he took the ultimate risk to prove his innocence to them [the friends] because he fully believed that God would act on these maledictions.[4]

As you review **Chapter 31**, watch for a conditional word that is used 13 times in *The New American Standard Bible Updated.*[5] What is the word?

Table 7.1 Job's oath of innocence

JOB'S OATH OF INNOCENCE		
VERSES	**"IF" SIN**	**CONSEQUENCES**
31:16-18	*Lack of care for the poor*	*Shoulder fall from socket and arm broken off at the elbow*

In table 7.1, list the conditional "if" sins and the subsequent consequences that Job was willing to undergo if doing so would vindicate him. There are at least ten, but you need *record* only *five*. Several may be grouped together under one heading and not all are introduced by "if." Remember that most of the book of Job is poetry, including chapter 31, and the images used can be vivid. *See the example.*

Not only is Chapter 31 Job's impassioned oath of innocence, it is his final discourse. "The words of Job are ended" (Job 31:40). Also included in that last verse is talk of briars and stinkweed for Job's land, a curse that Job was willing to welcome, yet a consequence he was adamant he would not face. Surely in his court case against God the matter of his innocence would be settled and briars and stinkweed would be ferreted out and burned!

REFLECTIONS ON LESSON 7

Truths I have learned that deepen my relationship with the Lord

Day 1

How do the two aspects of God's knowledge make Him the perfect Judge?

Day 2

Which of God's attributes may make Him seem distant from us?

Which of God's attributes may make Him seem near to us?

Day 3

Refute the idea that "God is not fair."

Refute the idea that it is okay to be angry at God because "He's big enough to take it."

Day 4

Describe the court scene, the players, the charges and the predicted verdict.

Day 5

What was the significance of Job's "if, then" oath of innocence in **chapter 31**?

Notes

1. Spiros Zodhiates, *Hebrew-Greek Key Word Study Bible* (Chattanooga, TN: AMG, 1990. Copyright 1984 and 1990 by AMG), 1726.

2. John Piper, Sermon on Romans 9:14-18, *The Fame of His Name and the Freedom of Mercy* (Bethlehem Baptist Church, Minneapolis, MN, February 2, 2003. Copyright 2003 with Permissions by Desiring God, on their website http://www.desiringgod.org/ResourceLibrary/Sermons/ByDate/2003. Accessed August 12, 2010).

3. G. Campbell Morgan, *The Answers of Jesus to Job* (Grand Rapids: Baker, 1973. Reprinted from the edition published in 1935 by Fleming H. Revell), 89.

4. Robert L. Alden, *The New American Commentary: Job* (Nashville: Broadman and Holman, 1993. Copyright 1993 by Broadman and Holman), 297.

5. *The Holy Bible Updated New American Standard Bible* (Grand Rapids: Zondervan, 1999. Copyright 1999 by Zondervan), 453-54.

LESSON 8 GOD'S JUSTICE

Day 1—God's Gracious Justice to the Wicked

Why do the wicked still live, Continue on, also become very powerful?
—Job 21:7

Assignment: 1. Read Job 21 and selected passages.
2. Record any meaningful scriptures in figures 0.2 through 0.4, the *Attributes of God* charts.

Job had been weighing the issue of justice and injustice and why the righteous suffer and the wicked prosper. As he compiled his case against God, he concluded that God was an unjust Judge. Until his own suffering, Job had agreed with his friends that God always punishes the guilty in this life. But in the midst of probing God's justice, Job puzzled over the difference between that view (Job 27) and his observation that the wicked prosper and often go unpunished. Throughout his discussions, he vacillated between the two views, causing some commentators to doubt that Job really was the speaker of all of chapter 27.[1] We, however, attribute the disparity to Job's quest for understanding of an enigmatic problem.

1. Read **Job 21:7-16** for Job's observation of the prosperity of the wicked.

7

8

9

10

11

12

13

Job witnessed the arrogant wicked rebel against and defy God, yet live "the good life" (21:14-15).

2. Job declared in 21:16 that the prosperity of the wicked is not by their hand. By whose hand do they prosper? Job faced a dilemma because he knew that God is sovereign and therefore obviously gives mercy to the wicked as well as to the righteous. Describe God's common grace, also called common mercy, from the following scriptures.

Matthew 5:45

Luke 6:35

Acts 14:16-17

Common grace can be defined as "the grace of God by which he gives people innumerable blessings that are not part of salvation."[2] Because Acts 14:17 states, "He did not leave Himself without witness," we understand the common graces of rains and fruitful seasons as one way God reveals Himself to all people. Even the most wicked of men benefit from these blessings, though they reject the Benefactor.

3. How does **Romans 2:4** explain God's redemptive purpose for common grace?

How patient and gracious is our God! Pray for someone you know who does not know Christ as their Savior, that the kindness of God will lead them to repentance.

Does the understanding of God's common grace give you a greater appreciation for His goodness? If so, how?

If you begrudge God's goodness to the wicked, take a moment to meditate upon the above verses and ask God to give you a heart like His.

Day 2—God's Delayed Justice of the Wicked

Why do the wicked still live, Continue on, also become very powerful?
—Job 21:7

Assignment: 1. Read Psalm 73 and selected passages.
2. Record any meaningful scriptures in figures 0.2 through 0.4, the *Attributes of God* charts.

Job's question, printed above, is as compelling to us as it was to him. The prosperous wicked "continue on" to this day, plaguing generations and challenging theologians. Psalm 73 expresses many of the same thoughts as in Job 21. Can you recall a time when you were as perplexed as Job? Have you been tempted to envy your unbelieving friends when they do well, receiving the favored jobs with bigger salaries, driving sportier cars, vacationing in places you have never been and shopping in elite stores instead of discount stores? The Psalmist also expresses perplexity about the apparent injustice of the wicked prospering; he envies those in his world. Read **Psalm 73** printed in table 8.1 and record the insights God gave the writer, including a satisfying new perspective on the LORD God. Next, answer the questions below.

Where is your focus?

Do you ever envy the wicked?

Do you need to confess that as sin and know the nearness of God as your greatest good?

After studying this portion of Job and Psalm 73, how would you answer the question of Job21:7?

Table 8.1 Psalm 73

PSALM 73 A Psalm of Asaph		
1	Surely God is good to Israel, To those who are pure in heart!	What was the psalmist's situation in verses 1-3?
2	But as for me, my feet came close to stumbling, My steps had almost slipped.	
3	For I was envious of the arrogant As I saw the prosperity of the wicked.	
4	For there are no pains in their death, And their body is fat.	How does the psalmist describe the prosperity of the wicked in verses 4-12?
5	They are not in trouble as other men, Nor are they plagued like mankind.	
6	Therefore pride is their necklace; The garment of violence covers them.	
7	Their eye bulges from fatness; The imaginations of their heart run riot.	
8	They mock and wickedly speak of oppression, They speak from on high.	
9	They have set their mouth against the heavens, And their tongue parades through the earth.	
10	Therefore his people return to this place, And waters of abundance are drunk by them.	
11	They say, "How does God know? And is there knowledge with the Most High?"	
12	Behold, these are the wicked; And always at ease, they have increased in wealth.	What thoughts in verses 13-14 did the psalmist have in common with Job in Job 9:29-30?
13	Surely in vain I have kept my heart pure And washed my hands in innocence;	
14	For I have been stricken all day long And chastened every morning.	
15	If I had said, "I will speak thus," Behold, I would have betrayed the generation of Your children.	
16	When I pondered to understand this, It was troublesome in my sight.	The psalmist pondered and was troubled about the prosperity of the wicked until . . . (verse 17):

Table 8.1 continued

#		
17 18	Until I came into the sanctuary of God; Then I perceived their end. Surely You set them in slippery places; you cast them down to destruction.	What understanding did the psalmist gain (verses 17-20)?
19	How they are destroyed in a moment! They are utterly swept away by sudden terrors!	
20	Like a dream when one awakes, O Lord, when aroused, You will despise their form.	
21	When my heart was embittered And I was pierced within,	The psalmist gave a before-and-after picture of himself in verses 21-24. How was he before hearing from God about the end of the wicked?
22	Then I was senseless and ignorant; I was like a beast before You.	
23	Nevertheless I am continually with You; You have taken hold of my right hand.	
24	With your counsel You will guide me, And afterward receive me to glory.	And after?
25	Whom have I in heaven but You? And besides you, I desire nothing on earth.	
26	My flesh and my heart may fail, but God is the strength of my heart and my portion forever.	This new understanding brought the psalmist into a deeper intimacy with the Lord. In the previous verses, the psalmist's focus had been on the wicked. Now where was his focus?
27	For, behold, those who are far from You will perish; You have destroyed all those who are unfaithful to You.	What did he know about God as a result (verses 23-28)?
28	But as for me, the nearness of God is my good; I have made the Lord GOD my refuge, That I may tell of all Your works.	

Day 3—God's Final Justice of the Wicked

This is the wicked man's portion from God, Even the heritage decreed to him by God.

—Job 20:29

Assignment: Read selected passages.

The Judge in Job's court case had not yet spoken. Eliphaz, Zophar and Bildad, self-appointed judges, clung to their guilty verdict of Job. Because of their "case closed" attitude, they believed that Job was suffering in this life because he was wicked.

Two significant questions, which you have studied, surfaced that spur debate until this day. Is God just? Why do the wicked prosper? In the flurry of thought and the fury of passions, in his desperate search to hear from God, Job was forced to contemplate another question: "What will happen to me after death?"

1. Job was firm and blunt in his opinion of what happens to all men at the end of life. Read **Job 3:11-19**.

   11-12 About what was Job complaining?

   13 Where did he say he would rather be?

   14-19 Who would be in his company?

Job believed in a destiny common to all mankind. How did he express this in **Job 21:26**?

Despite his lamenting that he didn't die at birth, Job was not happy about the prospect of death. Earlier in his suffering, he had complained that death was the only way for a righteous person to escape God's persecution (6:8-13; 7:1-21). But by **Job 16:22**, what was his mournful outlook?

2. Because Eliphaz, Zophar and Bildad had convicted Job of "wickedness to fellow man and to God," they had no doubt of Job's end: He would reap the portion of the wicked because he refused to repent. As they put forth their evidence, they watched Job go from despair to angry disparagement as he defended himself. Instead of retreating or softening their tone, the three applied more pressure.

Chapters **15**, **18** and **20** reveal what the three friends believed a wicked man should suffer. As you read the passages, notice the speakers' bleak pronouncements of finality for the wicked. Then record your findings in table 8.2 in one of three ways: summarize them, list them or illustrate them with simple drawings. If you draw, it will be helpful to remember that most of the book of Job is a poem rich with metaphors and similes. Your sketches can reflect these images from a poem about which has been said: "There is nothing written, I think, in the Bible or out of it, of equal literary merit." [3]

Job himself was not deficient in opinions of the portion of the wicked. (Again, keep in mind the poetic nature of the book of Job.) Job said that a wicked man's sons are destined for the sword; his descendants will not be satisfied with bread; others will divide his riches; his house is built like a spider's web; terrors overtake him like a flood; a tempest which he will try to flee will steal him away in the night; men will clap their hands and hiss at him in his place (Job 27:13-23).

Table 8.2 The portion of the wicked

THE PORTION OF THE WICKED		
Eliphaz Job 15:30-35	Bildad Job 18:5-21	Zophar Job 20:4-29

3. Job's anguished laments about the end of life and beyond echoed those of his friends. What he said in **Job 17:12-16** is an example. Read it and answer the questions below.

What images in verses **12** and **13** repeat those of the scriptures you completed in Question 2?

What was his physical body going to eventually become? (**16**)

To what place might he and his hope go? (**16**)

Throughout the Old Testament Sheol was described as follows:

- in biblical imagery, located down, beneath the surface of the earth as opposed to heaven, up above the earth where God dwells.[4]

- sometimes translated in American New Testaments by the Greek word *gehenna*—"hell" in English—indicating a place of final torment, normally a lake of fire. G*henna* was derived from the Old Testament Hebrew name for a narrow gorge near Jerusalem. It was the location of pagan worship and was eventually used as the city dump.[5] NOTE: Remember where Job was sitting (Job 2) in the land of Uz when his friends showed up to comfort him?

- sometimes described with images of death, smoke, fire and burning in or near the valley; linked with God's eternal portion for the wicked. If you would like to read more about this subject, the following passages are helpful: Isaiah 66:14-16, 24; Ezekiel 38-39; Joel 3:12-13 and Zechariah 14:12-15.

- inhabited. Who dwells in Sheol and for how long is largely a mystery left unexplained in scripture, although some hold that both Old Testament believers and the wicked are there.[6]

Many scholars agree that one of the clearest assessments of an afterlife in the Old Testament is found in **Daniel 12:1-4**, especially **verse 2**. What distinction is found between the two groups "who sleep in the dust of the ground"?

Sheol to Job was the unseen shadowy place or state of the dead, the "grave":

> Before I go—and I shall not return—To the land of darkness and deep shadow, The land of utter gloom as darkness itself, Of deep shadow without order, And which shines as the darkness.

> —Job, in Job 10:21-22

For Job, the afterlife was not sharply defined. What Job <u>could</u> count on was the finality of the grave. The troubles of this life cease and the physical body decays (Job 3:17-19). As Job contemplated his afterlife and demanded to hear from God, he could agree that, yes, one day his life would end and the worms would be his sister and mother. But more significantly, Job's gracious God, the all-sufficient One, had revealed Himself to Job before trials and troubles came (Job 1:8). Knowing Him allowed Job to recognize the portion of the wicked but confidently reject that end for himself: "Yet from my flesh I shall see God." Job continued to wait for His God to speak.

Do you personally know the same all-sufficient God that Job knew? Do you know if your portion will be with the wicked? Or will it be with the righteous? If you are not sure of your standing before God, turn now to Lesson 10 Day 5 for a helpful explanation about how you can know God through His Son, Jesus Christ.

Day 4—God's Active Justice

He . . . gives justice to the afflicted.

—Job 36:6

Assignment: 1. Read selected passages.

2. Record in figure 0.3, the *Attributes of God—Justice* chart.

Because God is just and right, He loves righteousness in His people (Isaiah 61:8). Old Testament righteousness took seriously one's obligations to God and others. Biblical justice is active and alert to the plight of those around them and shows compassion for the less fortunate or oppressed. Think about Job's life before God allowed him to be stricken (Job 29:12-17). He was a good example of one who stood up for justice. Today's study will focus on God's <u>active</u> justice.

1. What does **Job 36:6** indicate that God does for the afflicted?

According to the following verses, what specific acts of justice does God grant to the afflicted?

5:11

5:15

5:16

2. The New Testament carries forward the importance of active justice. What has been your response to the needs of the poor, the displaced, the ill, the widows and the fatherless? Compare your active justice to Job's. Table 8.3 is a three-columned chart titled *Active Justice*. The first column lists New Testament commands. In the second column, from **Job 29:12-17**, you are to describe how Job, thousands of years before the church age, showed God's righteousness and justice to others. The third column is for you to write your specific ideas for current or possible situations in your life. (The first entry on the chart is an example.) How <u>do</u> your intentions line up with Job's active justice?

Table 8.3 Job's active justice and yours

ACTIVE JUSTICE		
New Testament Commands	Job's Fulfillment of Active Justice In Job 29:12-17	Your Active Justice (Be Specific)
James 1:27 *Visit orphans and widows.* **1 Timothy 5:16** *Assist widows.*	*He delivered the poor and orphans.* 12	*Keep foster child until adoption.*
2 Corinthians 1:3-4 *Comfort.*	13	
Matthew 23:14 *Give justice to widows.*	14	
Matthew 23:23 *Show justice, mercy, faithfulness.*	14	
Luke 3:11 *Share clothes and food.*	16	
Luke 14:12-14 *Help the crippled, lame, blind.*	15	
Matthew 25:37-40 *Care for naked, hungry, stranger, prisoner and sick.*	16	
Romans 6:13 *Act as an instrument of righteousness.*	17	

How seriously are you pursuing active justice to show compassion for others? Prayerfully consider your responsibilities before God. How can you be more pleasing to Him in these areas?

For we are His workmanship, created in Christ Jesus for good works, which God prepared beforehand so that we would walk in them.

—Ephesians 2:10

Day 5—God's Active Justice in the Church

If I have despised the claim of my male or female slaves When they filed a complaint against me, What then could I do when God arises?

—Job 31:13

Assignment: Read selected scriptures.

Accused of mistreating the helpless, Job insisted that his own dealings with men had always been just and right. "Look at how I treated my slaves when they filed complaints against me," he argued in his great oath of innocence (Chapter 31). "How could I not judge them and their complaints fairly when I knew God was going to call me to account for my actions?"

Are we as sensitive as Job about being fair and just to others? Surely we must excel more than Eliphaz, Bildad and Zophar who acted not only as judges but as prosecutors, witnesses and jurors.

Leap forward in your imagination from Job's court case to our current day and Christian "judging." Picture a Bible-teaching local church. This church is blessedly made up of people who, by the power of the Holy Spirit, love and honor God. Even in such a wonderful setting, cases arise that require church leadership to make judgments according to biblical standards. More commonly, individual Christians in the body are called on to judge in the ordinary course of day-to-day living. One such Christian in the church – we will call her Mary– is aware that a fellow believer is ensnared in sin. Unlike Job's friends who talked and judged without knowledge, Mary knows her Christian friend's struggle. Is she to speak boldly with her friend about the sin? Or is she to keep silent?

First, she must consider the following command and its ramifications. "Do not judge so that you will not be judged" (Matthew 7:1) is a New Testament command often taken out of context and used as an excuse to avoid intervention. "I'm not going to be judgmental" is an expression heard today in both biblical and secular circles. One of the meanings of the Greek word *judge* in this context is "to form or express a judgment or opinion as to any person or thing, more commonly unfavorable." [7]

Is it acceptable—even expected—for Mary to confront her friend in terms the world would call "unfavorable"? God expects His people to be willing to judge each other rightly and properly. But he couples a strong caution with the command to judge. Jesus Christ forcefully spelled out the condition during His Sermon on the Mount.

1. Read **Matthew 7:1-5** and answer the questions to find out the prerequisite for judging.

[1] Do not judge so that you will not be judged.

[2] For in the way you judge, you will be judged; and by your standard of measure, it will be measured to you.

³ Why do you look at the speck that is in your brother's eye, but do not notice the log that is in your own eye?
⁴ Or how can you say to your brother, 'Let me take the speck out of your eye,' and behold, the log is in your own eye?
⁵ You hypocrite, first take the log out of your own eye, and then you will see clearly to take the speck out of your brother's eye.

—Matthew 7:1-5

2a In what way will you be judged?

2b What will the measuring standard be?

2b How will the standard be used?

3a How large is the impediment in your brother's eye?

3b How large is the impediment in your eye?

4a What do you offer to do for the brother?

4b What is wrong with that offer?

5a What are you instructed to do for yourself?

5b Then, what can you do for your brother?

From your understanding of the Matthew passage, what should Mary in our example do before confronting her friend about sin?

We are not told if Eliphaz, Bildad and Zophar examined themselves before they tore into Job. We can only assume that they believed that they had nothing of which to repent. We can only wonder at their audacious judgment of a friend.

Have you been reluctant to challenge a fellow Christian about sin in her life out of fear of being "judgmental"?

Have you missed opportunities to help a Christian because of unwillingness to deal with sin in your own life?

Have you misjudged and gossiped about others? Do you need to ask forgiveness from or make restitution to anyone?

2. There is a second important caution every Christian called upon to judge must heed from Galatians 6:1: "Brethren, even if anyone is caught in any trespass, you who are spiritual, restore such a one in a spirit of

gentleness; each one looking to yourself, so that you too will not be tempted." According to **Galatians 6:1**, after we have determined that it is biblically right to speak to a fellow believer ensnared in sin, what should be our attitude as we go?

What should be your goal?

Although Eliphaz may have begun his speech in a spirit of gentleness, he quickly joined the other two friends in their increasingly harsh accusations of Job. It does not appear that any of the three friends "looked to himself" in his verbal journey.

3. Later in Matthew 7, God helpfully provided additional insight into judging others. He did so through a command requiring that evaluation be made. Read about a tree and its fruit in **Matthew 7:15-20** and answer the questions. The passage targets one group of people, but its command to judge is applicable to all Christians.

15 We are to be on the lookout for whom?

15 How are they described?

16, 20 How are we to recognize them?

17-18 What comparisons did Matthew use?

What final judgment appears in **verse 19**?

Because God has called us to judge, He will equip us to do that work. Our obedience to Matthew 7:1-5 is to result in gentle rebuke and hopeful restoration for a sinning friend; our obedience to Matthew 7:15-20 is to be protection for the body of Christ and defense of God's Word and honor.

Poor Job. No gentle rebuke for him from three who were not concerned about the justness of the judgment they had meted out. He must wait for God's vindication.

REFLECTIONS ON LESSON 8

Truths I have learned that deepen my relationship with the Lord

Day 1

How does the doctrine of common grace answer the question in **Job 21:7**?

What is God's redemptive purpose in granting common grace (**Romans 2:4**)?

Day 2

What satisfying insight does God give to the writer of **Psalm 73** about the puzzle of the prosperous wicked?

Day 3

What was Job's opinion of the destiny of men at the end of life?

What metaphors are used to describe the portion of the wicked?

According to Job and his three friends, what is the portion of the wicked?

What part did Sheol play in Job's thinking about an afterlife?

Day 4

How does a right view of God's justice affect your ministry to others?

Day 5

When called upon to judge, how then does a Christian know if he is rightly doing so?

Matthew 7:15-20 tells of a tree and its fruit. What additional insight into judging others does that passage give us?

Notes

1. Roy B. Zuck, *JOB* (Chicago: Moody, 1978. Copyright 1978 by Moody Bible Institute of Chicago), 121.

2. Wayne Grudem, *Systematic Theology* (Leicester, England: Inter-Varsity, 1994. Copyright 1994 by Wayne Grudem), 1238.

3. Thomas Carlyle, "Heroes and Hero Worship, Lecture II, May 8, 1840, The Hero as Prophet, Mahomet: Islam," Public Domain.

4. Lawrence O. Richards, ed., *The Revell Bible Dictionary* (Old Tappan, NJ: Fleming H. Revell. Copyright 1990 by Fleming H. Revell), 914.

5. Richards, 480.

6. Richards, 914.

7. Spiros Zodhiates, *The Complete Word Dictionary* (Chattanooga, TN: AMG, 1992. Copyright 1992 by AMG, 1993 revised edition), 888.

LESSON 9
JOB'S RESPONSE TO GOD'S SILENCE

Day 1—Job's Response to God's Silence: Questioning

Have I sinned? What have I done to You, O watcher of men? Why have You set me as Your target?

—Job 7:20

Assignment: Read selected passages.

While Job's faith endured, he ranted and raved, rationalized and reasoned as he challenged God's justice and mercy. How <u>was</u> he going to be vindicated? If God would not speak to him, if God remained silent, how would his dilemma ever be resolved? This lesson will explore how Job moved from faultfinding with God and complaining to praising and trusting his all-sufficient God.

Job was bogged down in a "dark night of the soul," comfortless and without hearing from the "God of all comfort" (2 Corinthians 1:3). How long Job sought God before He answered him is unknown. Why does God delay in answering His servants when they call upon Him? Job never learned why, and often neither do we when we go through seasons of God's silence.

Sometimes God's silence is due to what is happening heavenward, the activity in the spiritual realm. Daniel, in the tenth chapter of the book of Daniel, earnestly sought understanding from God, mourning, fasting and humbling himself for three weeks with no answer. Finally an angel responded that "the prince of the kingdom of Persia was withstanding me for twenty-one days; then behold, Michael, one of the chief princes, came to help me, for I had been left there with the kings of Persia. Now I have come to give you an understanding" (Daniel 10:13-14). Surely, we must take seriously the apostle Paul's warning that "our struggle is not against flesh and blood, but against the rulers, against the powers, against the world forces of this darkness, against the spiritual forces of wickedness in the heavenly places" (Ephesians 6:12).

At other times, God is silent to develop intimacy with us. If Job had realized that God's silence would result in a deeper relationship with him, then he might have been able to pray, watch and wait, trusting his all-sufficient God to answer Him in His time and in His way. Instead, Job reacted to God's silence with depression, complaints and despair one moment and glimmers of hope the next.

1. In the face of God's silence, what was Job's first of several questions within **7:20**?

Job was correct to check his own heart for sin. Matthew Henry suggested that "when at any time we are under the sense of God's withdrawings, we are concerned to enquire into the reason of them—what is the sin for which he corrects us and what the good he designs us." [1] God had already established Job's integrity in chapters 1 and 2. Job's suffering and God's silence to him were <u>not</u> due to some unspecified sin he had committed prior to his suffering.

Read **Psalm 139:23-24**. *How might the prayer of the psalmist be helpful to you in times of God's silence?*

2. With God's continued silence, Job asked "Why?" What "why" questions did Job ask?

    3:20, 23

    10:2

    10:18

    13:24

There are those who insist that it is a very bad thing to question God. To them, "why?" is a rude question. That depends, I believe, on whether it is an honest search, in faith, for his meaning, or whether it is a challenge of unbelief and rebellion. The psalmist often questioned God and so did Job. God did not answer the questions, but he answered the man —with the mystery of himself.[2]

—Elisabeth Elliot

Is there a biblical way to question God without unbelief and rebellion as Elisabeth Elliot suggested? How is her idea that God is not as interested in answering all our questions as He is in revealing Himself consistent with **Hebrews 11:6**?

When will you seek God and find Him, according to **Jeremiah 29:12-13**?

Where are we to "search, in faith, for meaning," according to **Psalm 119:50**?

What "why?" questions do you have for God? How might you "search, in faith, for meaning"?

Day 2—Job's Response to God's Silence: Faultfinding

God has wronged me.

—Job 19:6

Assignment: 1. Read selected passages.
2. Record in table 9.1, the *Reframing Circumstances* chart, located at the end of today's assignment.

Job did have legitimate questions for God. Some of his complaints were valid. But some were not. Is there a biblical way to complain? Matthew Henry noted that we may complain <u>TO</u> God, but not <u>ABOUT</u> God: "It is intimated that those who quarrel with God, do, in effect, go about to teach him how to mend His work . . . He that contends with God is justly looked upon as his enemy."[3]

1. Some clear examples of Job complaining ABOUT God are found in **16:9-14 and 19:7-13, 22.**

What did he call God in **16:9?**

How did he describe God's anger against him?

   16:9

Where did he say God "tossed" him?

   16:11

What verbs did Job use to describe what God did to him?

   16:12

What attribute of God was <u>not</u> evident to Job?

   16:13

How did he picture God in **16:14?**

In **19:6-7**, Job declared, "God has _____ me…Behold, I cry 'Violence!' but I get no _____; I shout for help, but there is no _____."

2. You have already learned that in order to justify himself and maintain his own innocence, Job deduced that God is unjust.

What did the LORD call Job in **40:2?**

What was the Lord's rebuke in **40:8?**

We will study God's answer to Job and Job's repentance in depth later. The purpose for studying Job's faultfinding of God is to help us avoid the same sin. A. W. Pink wrote that questioning God's wisdom and right to test us is "wicked insubordination."[4] He referred to **Romans 9:20**. What does it say?

What warning does **Isaiah 45:9** give?

When Job doubted God's goodness, wisdom, love and justice, he cast aspersions upon the character of Creator God. How can we avoid "wicked insubordination" when we are under trial?

Many saints through the ages have learned how to gain a fresh, biblical perspective of their troubles. They reframed their complaints and circumstances. In other words, they changed how they looked at a circumstance. They replaced their complaints with responses that honored God. They often remembered God's mercies to them before and during their trials.

3. Reframing circumstances requires practice to do the following:

- Seek God in faith, for answers, trusting Him as your all-sufficient God (Job 13:3).
- Seek answers from God in His Word (Job 23:12).
- Remember God's lovingkindness (Job 10:12), and His other attributes relevant to your situation.
- Ask Him to give you His perspective of your circumstance (Job 7:20; Colossians 3:1-3).
- Be thankful to Him, submitting to His providential dealings in your life (Job 13:15).
- Bless His name (Job 1:21).

Think about reframing a circumstance in your life about which you might normally complain. What mercies has the Lord shown you in that area in the past? What mercies is He showing you now? Thank Him for withholding even worse circumstances. Thank Him for the strength He has provided during the trial. Thank Him for seeing you through the trial. Thank Him for growing you through the trial.

For further practice reframing circumstances, refer to table 9.1. Add to the list using the examples provided as a guide.

Table 9.1 Reframing circumstances

REFRAMING CIRCUMSTANCES	
Complaints from Job and Your Complaints	**Circumstances Reframed**
3:20, 23 Why is light given to him who suffers?	Though "my flesh and my heart fail . . . God is the strength of my heart and my portion forever" (Psalm 73:26). I can still please God. Even when it is difficult, I can be responsible (2 Corinthians 5:9; Romans 12:1-2).
13:24 Why do You hide Your face from me?	As tough as my situation is, I know that I am not alone. God's word promises that He will never leave me nor forsake me (Hebrews 13:5).
10:18 Why have You brought me out of the womb?	I was born to glorify God (Ephesians 1:4-6; Psalms 139:13-16).
16:13 Without mercy He splits my kidneys.	Even Jesus learned obedience by the things He suffered (Hebrews 5:8). God's will is to conform me to the image of His Son. He will work it out for my good and His glory (Romans 8:28-29).
30:21-22 God is being cruel to me.	This situation certainly seems dismal. But I know from God's Word that He is good (Psalm 34:8) and His lovingkindness endures forever (Psalm 118:1).
My husband . . .	
My children . . .	
My life . . .	
My church . . .	
My . . .	

Day 3—Job's Response to God's Silence: Praise

Behold, these are the fringes of His ways; And how faint a word we hear of Him! But His mighty thunder, who can understand?

—Job 26:14

Assignment: 1. Read selected passages.
                 2. Record in figures 0.2 through 0.4, the *Attributes of God* charts.

Job's dialogue was not filled with complaints only. He also considered God's workmanship in creation and praised God's attributes. At the beginning of his trials Job was able to bless the LORD. However, as the trials wore on, he experienced ups and downs in his faith while never losing his faith. When Job focused upon God and the "fringes of His ways" (Job 26:14), his hope resurged. Today you will enjoy three passages in which Job praised God's majesty.

Job 9:2-15

1. **Job 9:2-15** is Job's hymn to God as he contemplated how he could dispute with God successfully. What was the question in dispute?

    9:2

Some Bible students believe that Job was more concerned about proving himself right than being justified before God. How did Job express the futility of such a dispute with God?

    9:3

Job then proceeded to reason in **9:4-10** about how overpowering God is. The hymn sprang from Job's recognition of God's superiority and his own utter helplessness.

Paraphrase **9:4**: No one can compete with God's _____and

_____.

What did Job say about God's power and authority over the following?

    5 mountains

    6 foundations of the earth

    7 sun

    7 stars

    8 heavens

8 sea

9 constellations

According to Job, God causes chaos and upheaval (9:5-7a) as well as order (9:7b-9) in this universe. What conclusion did Job reach about God's majesty in **9:10** that Eliphaz had also concluded in **5:9**?

What three contrasts did Job make in **9:11-12** between his own powerlessness and God's omnipotence?

Job emphasized God's superior power by citing His power over the helpers of the ancient mythological sea monster Rahab. Because of God's advantages, what was Job's conclusion in **9:14-15**?

Choose a key verse from **Job 9:2-15** and write it below.

Job 12:7-25

2. Job's sense of powerlessness continued in **chapter 12** as he praised God's power over nature (7-12), man and providence (13-25). He suggested we call upon nature to teach us about God. Upon what in nature did Job recommend we call?

7-8

What does nature teach?

9-10

You should already be familiar with **12:13-25** from Lesson 6 Day 3 about God's providence. How have you recently seen God's providence working among men?

Job extolled God's omniscience in **12:22**: "He _____ _____ from the darkness, and brings deep darkness into _____."

Choose a key verse from **Job 12:7-25** and write it below.

Job 26:6-14

3. Job's sense of alienation from God gave way for a time to praising God's majestic ways. In this third passage of Job's praise to God, he expressed thought-provoking descriptions of creation that point to the Creator and cause us to marvel, *how did God do that and how does He continue to do that?* Match the following verses with the appropriate statement about God's rule over creation.

5	Nothing is revealed that God obscures.
6	Nothing is hidden that God uncovers.
7-8	Nothing is beyond God's encircling power and dominion.
9	Nothing is beyond God's rule, even the place of the departed spirits.
10-12	Nothing is beyond God's breath to clear up and His hand to subdue.
13	Nothing is beyond God's ability to stretch, wrap and hold together.

14 "Behold, these are the fringes of His ways; And how _____ a word we hear of Him! But His _____ _____who can understand?"

Choose a key verse from **Job 26:6-14** and write it below.

Optional:

Spend the rest of your study time today writing a tribute to God for His faint words and mighty thunder in your own life.

Day 4—Job's Response to God's Silence: Wisdom

*But where can wisdom be found? And where is the place of understanding?
. . . God understands its way, And He knows its place.*

—Job 28:12, 23

Assignment: 1. Read Job 28 and selected passages.
2. Record in figure 0.3, the *Attributes of God—Wisdom* chart.

Commentators would have classified the book of Job as wisdom literature without chapter 28; but its inclusion firmly establishes the wisdom designation. The biblical genre of wisdom literature includes writings that give practical advice and observations about wise and foolish men. Some writers view the chapter as out-of-place and disassociated from the third dialogue.[5] Yet, it seems appropriate for Job to remind himself of the value of seeking God and His wisdom in all circumstances.

1. In **Job 28**, Job compared the search for wisdom to mining for metal and gems. What metals did he name in **verses 1-2**?

Man penetrates _____ (3) and _____ (4-5) to find what treasures (6)?

To find treasures, man goes places unseen by _____ and not trodden by

_____ (7-8).

What methods of excavation are mentioned in **verses 9-11**?

With what result?

10b, 11b

Job then compared the tedious process of mining to the search for _____.

12

Where is wisdom not found?

13-14

Wisdom is so valuable it cannot be bought with what treasures?

15-19

From what is wisdom hidden?

20-22

Who alone knows the way and place of wisdom?

23

2. Job has described the diligence and determination necessary to seek wisdom from its Source. How does God in His sovereignty give or withhold wisdom, according to the passages below?

Job 38:36

Job 39:13-18

If we lack wisdom, what are we to do, according to the wisdom literature of the New Testament, the book of James, in **James 1:5**?

In contrast to God's dealings with the ostrich from which He withholds wisdom, how does God respond to those who seek wisdom from Him (**James 1:5**)?

3. What attribute of God is closely related to His wisdom?

Job 28:24

Job 28:25-27 From the beginning of creation, God in His wisdom "imparted _____ to the wind And meted out the waters by _____ . . . set a _____for the rain and a _____ for the thunderbolt."

Read **Job 38:37-38**. Keeping in mind that in literature, weather phenomena often represent the circumstances of life, what was God's message to Job in relating that He keeps count of the clouds by wisdom?

How did God define wisdom in **Job 28:28**?

God was teaching Job about His wise and purposeful involvement in Job's suffering. Job was learning a form of the definition of wisdom used in this study: God in His wisdom knows how to bring about His plan. He knows and does what is best, is omniscient or all-knowing, perfect in knowledge, and nothing is hidden from Him. Therefore, Job's search for wisdom in his suffering led him to the answer to persevere in fearing the Lord and trusting in His perfect wisdom.

Knowing that we must seek wisdom diligently, and that God is the Source of wisdom, is there a matter about which you need to ask God for wisdom?

Day 5—Job's Response to God's Silence: Hope

If a man dies will he live again? All the days of my struggle I will wait Until my change comes.

—Job 14:14

Assignment: 1. Read selected passages.
2. Record in figures 0.2 through 0.4, the *Attributes of God* charts.

In the book of James, Job is cited as an example of a patriarch who endured. Though he found fault with God, he did not renounce Him. Instead, time after time he returned to his whole-hearted devotion to God and exhibited enduring faith and hope. Today you will learn how Job put his theology into practice as he waited, trusted and hoped in the all-sufficient God. You will study three objects of Job's hope: perseverance under trial, vindication and resurrection.

1. In 17:9, Job included himself among the righteous who, "hold to his way" and "grow stronger and stronger." Instead of allowing suffering to estrange him from God, Job determined to deepen his relationship with Him. Such perseverance is reflected in words such as wait, trust and hope. All three of those words are used to translate the Hebrew word *yachal* (#3176) in the following verses. Write the verses and circle wait, trust or hope, depending upon which Bible version you use.

13:15

14:14

Are you among the righteous that grow stronger and stronger in their hope in God?
What declaration of hope can you make to your all-sufficient God?

In a glimmer of hope, Job envisioned a time when, after a lifetime of struggles, his change would come. The change would include conversation and fellowship initiated by God, who would long for Job, the work of His hands. The change would also include God's forgiveness of Job's sin, transgression and iniquity. The use of those three terms indicates a thorough cleansing (14:14-17).

Job's declaration of hope in **23:10-12** also had the idea of cleansing and purifying. Read the verses and identify phrases that indicate Job's hope for:

- vindication
- perseverance

2. Job was confident that his integrity would be proven by the testing he was undergoing. He exhibited further confidence in the following passage as he emphatically stated, "As for me, I know . . ." What did Job know so confidently in **19:25-27**? Read that passage and identify phrases that indicate Job's hope for:

- vindication
- resurrection

Look up the Hebrew word for redeemer, *ga'al* (#1350, also spelled go'el) and write the definition below.

Some scholars caution us to not apply our Christian understanding of redeemer to this passage in Job.[6] The Hebrew understanding of redeemer early on was that of a blood relative who would accomplish one or more of the following:

- champion the cause of a needy relative.
- redeem an enslaved relative and/or restore forfeited property.
- defend and vindicate a relative against injury or wrong suffered (especially in a lawsuit).
- avenge a murdered relative.
- marry a relative's childless widow to continue the family name.[7]

For example, Boaz became a kinsman redeemer for Ruth in Ruth 2:20. Redeemer became a more theological term in the psalms and prophetic books:

> The question is whether Job was using it in the older sense, hoping for some relative to stand up for him, or whether in the later sense that Yahweh was Israel's Redeemer.[8]

In the next lesson you will further explore Job's understanding of redeemer. At the very least Job longed for a vindicator who would deliver from affliction and wrong which was not due to sin. Job's desire was for <u>active</u> justice by a redeemer who would not be silent and do nothing, as he felt God had done, but would arise and take action to defend him.

3. Though many scholars consider verse 25 a prophecy of the Redeemer Jesus Christ who would save His people from their sins, Job's words in this passage probably indicate he was not so concerned about being delivered from his sins as he was in being defended for his integrity.[9] At this point he recognized such vindication might not come in his lifetime. What in **Job 19:26** indicates that Job believed that when his vindication finally did come, God Himself would reveal it to him?

What did Jesus promise the pure in heart in **Matthew 5:8**?

As children of God we are promised in **1 John 3:2** that when Christ appears, _____

_____.

Psalm 11:7 promises that the upright will _____.

The psalmist in **Psalm 17:15** expects to behold _____ and be

satisfied with _____.

What are you willing to forsake to be able to behold the face of God?

4. In 14:14 Job pondered, "If a man dies, will he live again? All the days of my struggle I will wait until my change comes." Job believed that "even after my skin is destroyed, yet from my flesh I shall see God" (19:26). Though Job had minimal understanding of a physical resurrection from the dead, he revealed a hope, a confidence in the all-sufficient God's provision even beyond the grave. What a marvelous glimpse of future glory, which the apostle Paul elaborated on with similar thoughts:

- Outer man is decaying, yet inner man is being renewed (2 Corinthians 4:16).
- The dead will be raised imperishable; we will be changed (1 Corinthians 15:52).
- Christ will transform the body of our humble state into conformity with the body of His glory (Philippians 3:20-21).

The concept of resurrection does not provide the key to unlock the mystery of Job's present suffering, but it does offer a framework for hope. Job's yearning later becomes conviction (19:25 ff.), and such a hope is glorious. This ultimate hope of redemption is not, however, the central theme of the Book of Job. The book does, indeed, challenge us to endure, with hope. But it confronts us with an even more profound demand. It sounds the primary and everlasting call for glad consecration, come what may, to the covenant Lord.[10]

5. You have studied this week how Job responded to God's silence at times with faultfinding against God, yet at other times with splendid hymns of praise. Comfortlessness was interspersed with consolations of hope. Job rejoiced, "in unsparing pain, That I have not denied the words of the Holy One" (6:10). Job's expression of joy was followed by the question, "What is my strength, that I should wait [*yachel*]? What is my end, that I should endure?" (6:11). Later he acknowledged that his perseverance was not by his own strength. In **10:12**, who did Job credit with preserving his spirit?

Where do you find strength to persevere under trial?

What scripture from today's study will help you hope, wait and trust God for perseverance, for vindication and resurrection?

REFLECTIONS ON LESSON 9

Truths I have learned that deepen my relationship with the Lord

Day 1

When was the last time you said, "God, where are you?"

Describe the circumstances and God's response.

What spiritual dangers can challenge a believer as he waits on God?

Day 2

What is a biblical way to question God without unbelief and rebellion?

Day 3

How can focusing on God's majesty engender hope?

For those who participated, share with the class the tribute to God that you wrote.

Day 4

Describe how God in His sovereignty dispenses wisdom.

Day 5

Using what you have learned from this lesson, discuss how to prepare yourself and put into practice what you believe about God when difficulty comes.

How does the hope of the resurrection encourage you to endure hardship?

Notes

1. *Matthew Henry's Commentary of the Whole Bible* (Peabody, MA: Hendrickson, 1991. Copyright 1991 by Hendrickson), 683.

2. Elisabeth Elliot, *Trusting God in a Twisted World* (Old Tappan, NJ: Fleming H. Revell, 1989. Copyright 1989 by Elisabeth Elliot), 18.

3. *Matthew Henry's Commentary of the Whole Bible*, 736.

4. Arthur W. Pink, *Tried by Fire* (North Little Rock, AR: Teaching Resources International, 2001. Copyright 2001 by Teaching Resources International), 6-7.

5. Roy B. Zuck, *JOB* (Chicago: Moody, 1978. Copyright 1978 by Moody Bible Institute of Chicago), 122-23.

6. Ralph Smith. *Job, A Study in Providence and Faith* (Nashville: Convention Press, 1971. Copyright 1971 by Convention Press), 81-82.

7. William Henry Green, *Conflict and Triumph* (Carlisle, PA: Banner of Truth Trust, 1999. Copyright 1999 by Banner of Truth Trust), 94.

8. Robert L. Alden, *The New American Commentary: Job* (Nashville: Broadman and Holman, 1993. Copyright 1993 by Broadman and Holman), 207.

9. Smith, 82.

10. Pfeiffer, Charles F. and Everett F. Harrison, ed., *The Wycliffe Bible Commentary* (Chicago: Moody, 1990. Copyright 1962 by Moody Bible Institute of Chicago), 473-74.

LESSON 10 JOB: FAITH

Day 1—Job: Old Testament Faith, Genesis 3

Though He slay me, I will hope in Him.

—Job 13:15

Assignment: Read selected scripture passages and answer questions.

At the beginning of his trials, Job blessed the LORD. As time wore on and the friends hammered away at Job's insistence of his righteousness, Job experienced ups and downs in faith. Despite God's silence, Job did not abandon faith in his all-sufficient God. Job could affirm hope despite persecution, terrible losses and abandonment by his remaining family. "Though he slay me, I will hope in Him." This declaration, a quick flash of light in Job's otherwise dark soliloquy, has been called one of the few positive statements of faith from Job's lips. As he clung to hope and faith in God, Job longed for a vindicator, a redeemer, who would deliver him from suffering which was not due to sin.

Commentator John MacArthur agrees that Job was ready to go to his death trusting God. He wrote that Job would persistently defend his innocence before God, "and was confident that he was truly saved and not a hypocrite."[1] Job declared in 13:16 (NKJV) that "He also shall be my salvation, for a hypocrite could not come before Him." What made Job's declaration possible? Consider the question in a broad sense: How were Job—and other Old Testament people—saved from God's judgment?

OLD TESTAMENT SALVATION – PRETEST

Before probing Old Testament salvation in this assignment and the next three, <u>record how you would now answer the question: How was Job saved?</u> The exercise is important because you will want to compare your answer to your post-study knowledge.

Figure 10.1. Knowledge of Old Testament salvation pretest

1. Begin your examination by revisiting the Garden of Eden, post-Fall. There we find God, Adam, Eve and the serpent. Adam is blaming Eve for his eating forbidden fruit from the tree of the knowledge of good and evil. Eve is blaming the serpent for deceiving her. God responds. What does the LORD God say to the serpent?

Genesis 3:14

After God curses the serpent's body, He curses him in another way. Write **verse 15**.

<u>You have just written what most Bible scholars and theologians for hundreds of years agree is the first gospel message of the Bible, the first promise of a savior from God's judgment of the everlasting consequences of sin, passed down through Adam to Job and the entire human race.</u> Now, in the 21st century, Christians embrace Jesus Christ, born several thousand years after Job probably lived, as Mediator, the Son of God whom God sent to save men from His wrath, spiritual death and hell.

The following New Testament scriptures reinforce and expound Genesis 3:15, the greatest of God's promises and provisions:

- The <u>serpent's (Satan's) seed</u> is his offspring. Satan is the father of lies, who speaks from his own nature. All people are by nature sinners, like Adam, the one by whom sin entered the world (John 8:44, Romans 5:12 and Hebrews 2:14).
- The <u>woman </u>is Eve, who was deceived by Satan's craftiness (2 Corinthians 11:3).
- <u>Eve's seed</u> is ultimately Jesus Christ (Luke 1:30-33; Acts 2:22-25), the Son of God and the One who takes away the sins of the world.
- Jesus Christ <u>bruised</u> Satan by <u>crushing</u> him under his feet (Romans 16:20). Jesus Christ rendered Satan powerless, who had the power of death.
- Satan <u>bruised</u> Jesus Christ in the heel by tempting Him—without success—to worship him. Jesus was resurrected from the dead after subjugating authorities and powers, including Satan, to Himself (Matthew 4:1-10; 1 Peter 3:18-22; 4:8-11).

Summarize the truth of **Genesis 3:15** in your own words.

2. Now that Adam had sinned by not believing God's Word, he fell under God's condemnation. Adam had transgressed God's moral law in his action and attitude, for God had made it clear that eating from the tree of the knowledge of good and evil would result in death (Genesis 2:17). Adam was banished from the garden, denied God's presence and separated from fellowship with God.

Why can God have no other view of sin than to hate it? Look up **Deuteronomy 32:4 (KJV)** and **Romans 1:18**. Find at least five reasons why God hates sin.

1.

2.

3.

4.

5.

How did Adam's sin affect Job, the man from Uz, who lived a thousand years or so after Adam? It affected Job the same way it affected every human born after Adam. It affected Job the same way it affects you. "Therefore, just as through one man (Adam) sin entered into the world, and death through sin, and so death spread to all men, because all sinned—" (Romans 5:12). In your study tomorrow, you will meet other Old Testament sinners like Job, pre-Jesus Christ and men with saving faith, who followed hard after God.

Day 2—Job: Old Testament Faith, Hebrews 11

Though He slay me, I will hope in Him.

—Job 13:15

Assignment: 1. Read Hebrews 11, printed in this lesson, and mark words as indicated.
2. Look up the words *faith, assurance and conviction* in a Bible reference book.

"Upright" Job shared inherited sin with Adam. If he had been left to his own strength and uprightness, Job would have had no hope of reconciliation with his God. But God in grace and mercy has selected people throughout history to believe in his promise of a "seed" who would deliver men from sin's penalty of death. Faithful people like Job are remembered in the New Testament book of Hebrews, acknowledged as the Bible's magnificent "roll call of faith." The list begins with Abel, one of Adam's sons. Abel and all the others, named and unnamed, are Old Testament examples of people whom God accepted because of their faith in Him and His word, which included His promises.

Although Job is not listed by name in the roll call, he affirmed similar faith by declaring that though God slew him, he would hope in God (Job 13:15). Like Job, the first four men commended—Abel, Enoch, Noah and Abraham—were men who "For by it (faith), men of old gained approval" (Hebrews 11:2). The four are essential examples whom God used to help us understand salvation in the Old Testament. And Job? He shares with Noah the privilege of being called "righteous and blameless" by God (Job 1:1; Genesis 6:9).

1. Chapter 11 of Hebrews begins with God's definition of faith. "Now faith is the assurance of things hoped for, the conviction of things not seen." It will be helpful to look up three key Greek words in the definition: faith, assurance and conviction. (You may want to refer to *A Word About Basic Word Study* located in the front of your study guide.) Use an expository dictionary and write the meanings below.

Faith (# 4102, general meaning)

Assurance (substance #5287 KJV)

Conviction (evidence #1650 KJV)

Using the information you recorded, write an expanded version of Hebrews 11:1. This exercise can give you an exceptional idea of God's wonderful, saving grace toward his people.

2. Keeping your expanded definition in mind, read **Hebrews 11** printed below. <u>Underline</u> the words *faith, promise, believe* and *righteousness*, each with a different color.

¹ Now faith is the assurance of things hoped for, the conviction of things not seen. ² For by it the men of old gained approval. ³ By faith we understand that the worlds were prepared by the word of God, so that what is seen was not made out of things which are visible. ⁴ By faith Abel offered to God a better sacrifice than Cain, through which he obtained the testimony that he was righteous, God testifying about his gifts, and through faith, though he is dead, he still speaks.

⁵ By faith Enoch was taken up so that he would not see death; AND HE WAS NOT FOUND BECAUSE GOD TOOK HIM UP; for he obtained the witness that before his being taken up he was pleasing to God. ⁶ And without faith it is impossible to please Him, for he who comes to God must believe that He is and that He is a rewarder of those who seek Him. ⁷ By faith Noah, being warned by God about things not yet seen, in reverence prepared an ark for the salvation of his household, by which he condemned the world, and became an heir of the righteousness which is according to faith. ⁸ By faith Abraham, when he was called, obeyed by going out to a place which he was to receive for an inheritance; and he went out, not knowing where he was going. ⁹ By faith he lived as an alien in the land of promise, as in a foreign land, dwelling in tents with Isaac and Jacob, fellow heirs of the same promise; ¹⁰ for he was looking for the city which has foundations, whose architect and builder is God. ¹¹ By faith even Sarah herself received ability to conceive, even beyond the proper time of life, since she considered Him faithful who had promised. ¹² Therefore there was born even of one man, and him as good as dead at that, as many descendants AS THE STARS OF HEAVEN IN NUMBER, AND INNUMERABLE AS THE SAND WHICH IS BY THE SEASHORE.

¹³ All these died in faith, without receiving the promises, but having seen them and having welcomed them from a distance, and having confessed that they were strangers and exiles on the earth. ¹⁴ For those who say such things make it clear that they are seeking a country of their own. ¹⁵ And indeed if they had been thinking of that country from which they went out, they would have had opportunity to return. ¹⁶ But as it is, they desire a better country, that is, a heavenly one. Therefore God is not ashamed to be called their God; for He has prepared a city for them.

¹⁷ By faith Abraham, when he was tested, offered up Isaac, and he who had received the promises was offering up his only begotten son; ¹⁸ it was he to whom it was said, "IN ISAAC YOUR DESCENDANTS SHALL BE CALLED." ¹⁹ He considered that God is able to raise people even from the dead, from which he also received him back as a type. ²⁰ By faith Isaac blessed Jacob and Esau, even regarding things to come. ²¹ By faith Jacob, as he was dying, blessed each of the sons of Joseph, and worshiped, leaning on the top of his staff. ²² By faith Joseph, when he was dying, made mention of the exodus of the sons of Israel, and gave orders concerning his bones.

²³ By faith Moses, when he was born, was hidden for three months by his parents, because they saw he was a beautiful child; and they were not afraid of the king's edict. ²⁴ By faith Moses, when he had grown up, refused to be called the son of Pharaoh's daughter, ²⁵ choosing rather to endure ill-treatment with the people of God

than to enjoy the passing pleasures of sin, ²⁶considering the reproach of Christ greater riches than the treasures of Egypt; for he was looking to the reward. ²⁷ By faith he left Egypt, not fearing the wrath of the king; for he endured, as seeing Him who is unseen. ²⁸ By faith he kept the Passover and the sprinkling of the blood, so that he who destroyed the firstborn would not touch them. ²⁹ By faith they passed through the Red Sea as though they were passing through dry land; and the Egyptians, when they attempted it, were drowned. ³⁰ By faith the walls of Jericho fell down after they had been encircled for seven days. ³¹ By faith Rahab the harlot did not perish along with those who were disobedient, after she had welcomed the spies in peace. ³² And what more shall I say? For time will fail me if I tell of Gideon, Barak, Samson, Jephthah, of David and Samuel and the prophets, ³³ who by faith conquered kingdoms, performed acts of righteousness, obtained promises, shut the mouths of lions, ³⁴ quenched the power of fire, escaped the edge of the sword, from weakness were made strong, became mighty in war, put foreign armies to flight. ³⁵ Women received back their dead by resurrection; and others were tortured, not accepting their release, so that they might obtain a better resurrection; ³⁶ and others experienced mockings and scourgings, yes, also chains and imprisonment. ³⁷ They were stoned, they were sawn in two, they were tempted, they were put to death with the sword; they went about in sheepskins, in goatskins, being destitute, afflicted, ill-treated ³⁸ (men of whom the world was not worthy), wandering in deserts and mountains and caves and holes in the ground.
³⁹ And all these, having gained approval through their faith, did not receive what was promised, ⁴⁰ because God had provided something better for us, so that apart from us they would not be made perfect.

—Hebrews 11

Do you have the faith of a Job, an Abel, an Enoch, a Noah? Look back at the words you emphasized by marking. Can you list at least two biblical truths about faith, promise, believe *and* righteousness *that confirm your faith in God, His Word and His promises? An example is: Abraham's wife Sarah believed God faithful to accomplish what He had promised to them, a son. I also can trust in His promises.*

Job suffered, yet his faith did not. Tomorrow you will learn about a man who, like Job, is a model of faith. He, like Job, was a man of good works. What did those works have to do with his salvation?

Day 3—Job: Old Testament Faith, Romans 4

Though He slay me, I will hope in Him.

—Job 13:15

Assignment: Read Romans 4 printed in this lesson.

Before being stricken and banished to the dung heap, Job had been a man of exemplary good deeds and kindnesses to his family, to his servants and to the people of his town in Uz (Job 29). He had sat as a chief at the city gates, giving opinions and rulings and comforting those in mourning.

Did the good deeds Job performed contribute to the reckoning of His salvation in God's eyes? To understand the role in salvation of being a "good person," we look at a New Testament passage about one of Job's possible contemporaries, Abraham, the Hebrew patriarch. Abraham also was a man of good works, a benevolent leader who built altars and shepherded his family.

Chapter 4 of the book of Romans lifts up Abraham as a man of faith. When Romans was written, Jewish descendants of Abraham believed that salvation was a result of a person's works plus faith. The Romans passage was written to refute the predominant and widely-accepted Jewish view. After you have observed and answered questions from Romans 4, you will have a decisive answer for contemporary "good persons" who are depending on works or works plus something for access to heaven.

Thoughtfully and carefully read the twenty-five verses of **Romans 4** printed for you below. Then read all the statements that follow the passage before writing your answers. Specific instructions for answering are located at the beginning of the questions.

[1]What then shall we say that Abraham, our forefather according to the flesh, has found?
[2] For if Abraham was justified by works, he has something to boast about, but not before God.
[3] For what does the Scripture say? "ABRAHAM BELIEVED GOD, AND IT WAS CREDITED TO HIM AS RIGHTEOUSNESS."
[4] Now to the one who works, his wage is not credited as a favor, but as what is due.
[5] But to the one who does not work, but believes in Him who justifies the ungodly, his faith is credited as righteousness,
[6] just as David also speaks of the blessing on the man to whom God credits righteousness apart from works:
[7] "BLESSED ARE THOSE WHOSE LAWLESS DEEDS HAVE BEEN FORGIVEN, AND WHOSE SINS HAVE BEEN COVERED.
[8] "BLESSED IS THE MAN WHOSE SIN THE LORD WILL NOT TAKE INTO

ACCOUNT."

⁹ Is this blessing then on the circumcised, or on the uncircumcised also? For we say, "FAITH WAS CREDITED TO ABRAHAM AS RIGHTEOUSNESS."

¹⁰ How then was it credited? While he was circumcised, or uncircumcised? Not while circumcised, but while uncircumcised;

¹¹ and he received the sign of circumcision, a seal of the righteousness of the faith which he had while uncircumcised, so that he might be the father of all who believe without being circumcised, that righteousness might be credited to them,

¹² and the father of circumcision to those who not only are of the circumcision, but who also follow in the steps of the faith of our father Abraham which he had while uncircumcised.

¹³ For the promise to Abraham or to his descendants that he would be heir of the world was not through the Law, but through the righteousness of faith.

¹⁴ For if those who are of the Law are heirs, faith is made void and the promise is nullified;

¹⁵ for the Law brings about wrath, but where there is no law, there also is no violation.

¹⁶ For this reason it is by faith, in order that it may be in accordance with grace, so that the promise will be guaranteed to all the descendants, not only to those who are of the Law, but also to those who are of the faith of Abraham, who is the father of us all,

¹⁷ (as it is written, " A FATHER OF MANY NATIONS HAVE I MADE YOU") in the presence of Him whom he believed, even God, who gives life to the dead and calls into being that which does not exist.

¹⁸ In hope against hope he believed, so that he might become a father of many nations according to that which had been spoken, "SO SHALL YOUR DESCENDANTS BE."

¹⁹ Without becoming weak in faith he contemplated his own body, now as good as dead since he was about a hundred years old, and the deadness of Sarah's womb;

²⁰ yet, with respect to the promise of God, he did not waver in unbelief but grew strong in faith, giving glory to God,

²¹ and being fully assured that what God had promised, He was able also to perform.

²² Therefore IT WAS ALSO CREDITED TO HIM AS RIGHTEOUSNESS.

²³ Now not for his sake only was it written that it was credited to him,

²⁴ but for our sake also, to whom it will be credited, as those who believe in Him who raised Jesus our Lord from the dead,

²⁵ He who was delivered over because of our transgressions, and was raised because of our justification.

—Romans 4

As you read over the statements below that refer to **Romans 4**, notice that your goal is to determine the truth of each statement. **Mark a T** for true statements and **an F** for false ones. Then correct the statements that are wrong by writing the biblical truth beneath the false statement. The first one is answered for you.

2 Abraham boasted before God about his works. __F__

Abraham did not boast before God about his works.

4 When he worked for God, his wages were his just due. _____

5 Works are always tied to righteousness. _____

5 Righteousness is credited to one who believes in Him who justifies the ungodly. _____

6 David said that works are blessed as righteousness. _____

7, 8 The LORD does not take into account the sins of the righteous. _____

10-11 God counted Abraham's circumcision as righteousness. _____

13-16 Abraham was counted righteous by keeping the Law. _____

15 The Law brings about faith. _____

16 Faith, in accordance with grace, saved Abraham and all those of like faith. _____

17-20 With respect to his old body and promised heir, Abraham had moments of wavering in unbelief. _____

20 Abraham's belief in the promise of God was a one-time event. _____

21 Abraham believed that what God had promised, God would do. _____

22 Abraham's faith in God was credited to him as righteousness. _____

23-25 Faith in God like Abraham's was strictly for Old Testament salvation. _____

Did you find and correct eight false statements?

God counted Abraham's belief in Him, His words and His promises as righteousness, the same that he did for Job and for all those listed in Hebrews 11. Both Job and Abraham were men devoted to doing good works, yet their deeds were as filthy rags to God (Isaiah 64:6). Their works were not credited to them as righteousness—their faith was. Other Bible passages (Titus 2:14, 3:8; James 2:26) assure us that good works are an outgrowth of faith, not the other way around.

Has today's study about faith and works increased your understanding about salvation by faith in the Old Testament? If so, how?

Day 4—Job: Old Testament Faith, Redeemer

And as for me, I know that my Redeemer lives.

—Job 19:25

Assignment: Write in figure 10.2 an explanation of how God saved Job and others like him in the Old Testament.

Job, the man from the land of Uz, isn't listed by name in the Hebrews 11 "roll call" of faith. Yet we know that God said this about him: "Have you considered My servant Job? For there is no one like him on the earth, a blameless and upright man, fearing God and turning away from evil?" (Job 1:8). We know, too, that although Job did good works, he did not rely on them to gain what he thought was God's lost favor.

For the last 2,000 years, when a Christian has referred to his Redeemer, he has meant God's Son, Jesus Christ. But for Job, *my Redeemer* meant God, who personally revealed Himself to Job as He did to other ancient patriarchs, including Abraham. Job cried out to God: "As for me, I know that my Redeemer lives" (Job 19:25a). Many biblical scholars carefully interpret Job 19:25 within the framework of what theologians call *progressive revelation.*[2] The term represents God's choosing to reveal, over time and through history, more and more specifics about Himself and about the woman's seed (Jesus Christ), introduced to Adam and Eve after the Fall. (See Day 1 of this lesson.)

In all of Job's soliloquy, his impassioned embrace of his Redeemer was the apex of his faith. Chapter 19 records that Job spoke those words of confidence in spite of a tormented soul (2), fear of God's "injustice" (7-10), loneliness (13-19) and physical suffering (20). Yet out of his despair, Job could further proclaim his faith in God by crying, "and at the last He will take His stand on the earth" (Job 19:25b).

Job's belief held future and eternal implications for him. "Even after my skin is destroyed, yet from my flesh I shall see God; Whom I myself shall behold, and whom my eyes will see and not another. My heart faints within me!" (Job 19:26-27). The MacArthur Study Bible expounds on these two verses. "Job had no hope left for this life, but was confident that 'after' he was dead, his Redeemer would vindicate him in the glory of a physical ('in my flesh') resurrection in which he would enjoy perfect fellowship with the Redeemer. That Jesus Christ is that Redeemer is the clear message of the gospel."[3]

By now in your study, you should have sufficient biblical information to form your own statement of Old Testament salvation. Draw on what you have learned. Be sure to include why people throughout history have needed saving. Consider God's first and only provision to take away sin and to appease His wrath against it. You may include examples from Hebrews 11. You may want to include some of the following key words: *Adam, Eve, sin, God's wrath, Seed, salvation, Satan, belief (faith), God's promise, Savior, saved from wrath, and progressive revelation.*

Word your explanation so that you can memorize it and share it with others.

OLD TESTAMENT SALVATION
How God saved His people from His eternal judgment

Figure 10.2. Explanation of Old Testament salvation

Turn back to Lesson 10 Day 1 and read the statement of Old Testament salvation that you wrote. In what points does the salvation statement you formulated above compare to your initial idea from Day 1?

Day 5—Faith: Old and New Testament, Mediator

Even now, behold, my witness is in heaven, And my advocate is on high... O that a man might plead with God As a man with his neighbor!
—Job 16:19, 21

Assignment: Write in figure 10.4 an explanation of New Testament salvation.

You have learned that throughout his physical, mental and spiritual anguish, Job held on to faith in his all-sufficient God. "Sinner, repent!" insisted his friends. But Job persisted in his conviction that God would vindicate him at the conclusion of the court case he "filed" against God. However, as you have learned, during the trial he needed and longed for an advocate, a mediator to provide access to God. Job knew that a godless man could not go before His presence (Job 13:16). Job lamented: "There is no mediator between us who may lay his hand upon us both" (Job 9:33).

Job's need was the need of all mankind, to have a mediator between himself and God who opens access to heaven and provides reconciliation with the God of perfect justice and mercy.

For generations, we have had the blessing of knowing exactly who that advocate is, Jesus Christ, the One whom God appointed from eternity past. As God's history in time and space unfolded, so did God progressively reveal specifics about His appointed mediator. He is the fulfillment of Genesis 3:15, a mediator born of woman who would crush Satan and his schemes. He is the Son of God. He is God's appointed One whose virgin birth, sinless life, substitutionary death on the cross and subsequent resurrection and ascension qualified Him to save us from God's wrath against sin. It is by faith in Jesus Christ's work on the cross that all men of all time must come for salvation. Holy God's plan to reconcile sinful man to Himself has forever been the same (Acts 17:30-31).

1. Those of us in this study may come from all types of religious backgrounds that espouse various beliefs about ways and paths to God. In the list below, mark any you understand to be essential to salvation.

_____ I give money to the church.	_____ I support worthy charities.
_____ I walked the aisle of a church.	_____ I go to confession.
_____ I have been baptized.	_____ I went to Sunday school as a child.
_____ I prayed "the sinner's prayer."	_____ I am a member of a church.
_____ I had a relative who was a preacher.	_____ I do my best to keep the Ten Commandments.
_____ I practice the Golden Rule.	_____ I do good works for others.

Compare your assessment of salvation essentials to the following illustration. What conclusion does it draw?

I give money to the church.
I support worthy charities.
I walked the isle of a church.
I go to confession.
I was baptized
I went to Sunday school as a child.
I prayed "the sinner's prayer."

I am a member of a church.
I had a relative who was a preacher.
I do my best to keep the Ten Commandments.

REJECTED

Ephesians 2:8-9: "For by grace you have been saved through faith; and that not of yourselves, it is the gift of God; not as a result of works, so that no one may boast."

Acts 4:12: "And there is salvation in no one else; for there is no other name [Jesus Christ] under heaven that has been given among men by which we must be saved."

Figure 10.3. Rejected ways to salvation vs. the one accepted Mediator

God's Word rejects the actions listed above as having any merit to make a sinner acceptable to God. What is our spiritual condition as sinners, separated from God?

Ephesians 2:1

Psalm 53:1-3

Finish this statement: We do not seek after God because

2. God's Word counters false and sinful actions and beliefs for true salvation by declaring Jesus Christ's credentials, His qualifications and His actions. Read the following scriptures and record your findings.

Who is Jesus Christ?

John 1:1-3, 14

How is Jesus Christ different from all other men?

Matthew 1:23

2 Corinthians 5:21

What does this qualify Him to be for us?

Isaiah 53:5-6

As our substitute, what did Jesus do for us?

1 Peter 3:18

How did God prove that Jesus was His appointed standard for judging the world?

Acts 17:31

What Jesus did for us and how He did it is called the *gospel*, the good news. What are three main points of the gospel?

1 Corinthians 15:1-4

How do we have eternal life in Christ Jesus?

Romans 6:23

Jesus' death on the cross in our place satisfied (propitiated) God's demands for righteousness and justice and appeased God's wrath against sin. Through Christ's sacrifice, God maintained His justice and at the same time justified those who have faith in Jesus Christ.

3. Because we are sinners, unable to do anything on our own to save ourselves from God's wrath, in what ways must God initiate?

John 6:44

Ephesians 2:5

How does He do that?

Ephesians 2:8-9

4. God gives a person faith to believe that Jesus is His Son who died on the cross in our place (Romans 10:9-10). To what does He call us? What does He enable us to do?

Acts 17:30

Acts 16:31

Romans 10:9-10

What does Christ promise?

John 6:37

5. What are the everlasting results of God-given belief in Jesus Christ, our mediator? Complete the following statements and rejoice in a good God who has given His people better-than-rock-solid assurance of eternity with Him.

Acts 3: 19 Your sins

Romans 8:1 You are no longer

Romans 8:1 You are in

Romans 8:15 You have received

2 Corinthians 5:17 You are

Ephesians 2:13, 14 You have been

How much greater is God's plan of salvation for us than any plan of our own! What greater act could God have done than saving man to glorify Himself? What greater act could God have done than to save us from eternity in hell, separated from Him? What greater act could God have done than to exercise His righteous judgments by providing a substitute for our death? What greater act could God have done than to provide a mediator between Himself and humans? What greater act could God have done than staying true to His character of holiness as He redeemed sinful man?

What expectation of seeing God after death do you have?

Do you know confidently that you are adopted into God's family, saved from the penalty of sin and reconciled to God through Christ's blood?

God considered Job His very own. God gave Job faith to fear Him, to trust Him, to treasure His Word "more than my necessary food" (Job 23:12) and to long for a mediator (Job 16:19, 21). Ultimately, He gave Job hope to one day see God with his own eyes (Job 19:25-27). In His Word, God promises that believers (both Old Testament and New Testament) will see Him face to face. We will serve God and rule with Him forever (Revelation 22:3-5).

6. Yesterday, you wrote an explanation of Old Testament faith. Now, using the information you have learned today, write an explanation of New Testament faith. Your goal for this exercise is to be able to clearly tell others about salvation through Jesus Christ alone. You may use the following key words as a guide: *Mediator, God's unchanging plan, faith, substitute, gift, helpless, dead in trespasses and sin, repent, believe, results, child of God, heaven.*

NEW TESTAMENT FAITH

How God saved His people from His eternal judgment

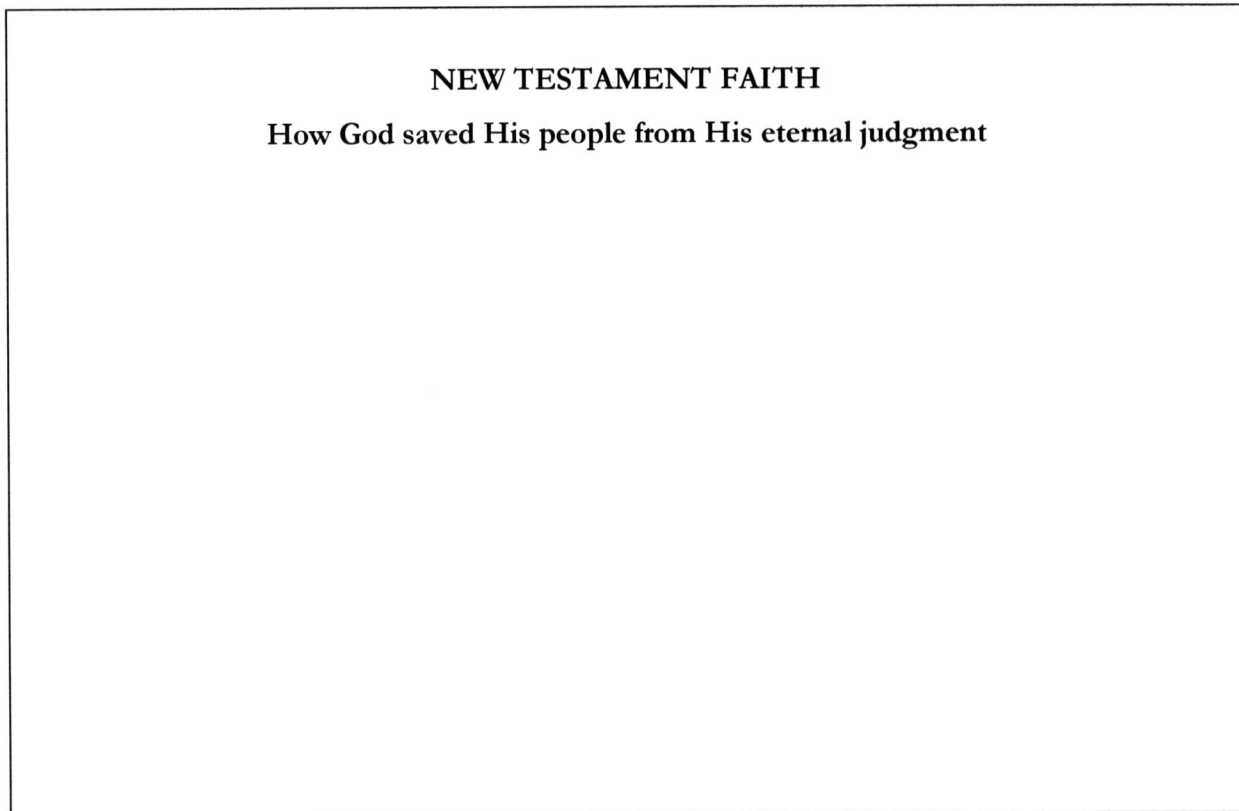

Figure 10.4. Explanation of New Testament Faith

Do you have a compelling desire to tell others the good news about salvation through Jesus Christ? Ask the Lord for an opportunity to share Christ with one person this week.

If you have questions about true salvation or have been convinced that you are not a Christian, do not delay in contacting a person who loves God and can share the good news more fully with you.

REFLECTIONS ON LESSON 10

Truths I have learned that deepen my relationship with the Lord

Day 1

What is the importance of **Genesis 3:15**?

How did Adam's sin affect Job?

How does Adam's sin affect us?

How are the concepts of *faith, belief* and *righteousness* relevant to Old Testament salvation?

Day 2

Why has Abraham been called a model person of faith?

What did Abraham find to be true about faith, belief and righteousness, according to **Romans 4**?

Day 3

Even though Job is not listed in the Hebrews 11 "roll call," how do we know Job was a man of faith?

Day 4

Share your written Old Testament plan of salvation from figure 10.2 with another member of your class.

Day 5

What need did Job have that is true for all mankind?

Explain why Job did not have faith specifically in the Lord Jesus Christ.

What kinds of plans do people make to try to mediate with God on their own?

What is God's one and only plan for salvation?

Share your New Testament plan of salvation from figure 10.4 with another member of the class.

Notes

1. John MacArthur, *The MacArthur Study Bible* (Nashville: Word, 1997. Copyright 1997 by Word), 711.

2. Walter A. Elwell, ed. *Baker Theological Dictionary of the Bible* (Grand Rapids: Baker, 1996. Copyright 1996 by Baker), 735.

3. MacArthur, 717.

LESSON 11 ELIHU

Day 1—Elihu: A Refreshing Voice

Indeed, there was no one who refuted Job, Not one of you who answered his words... I too will answer my share.

—Job 32:12, 17

Assignment: Read Elihu's words in chapters 32-37. Carefully note punctuation marks that indicate when Elihu quotes Job.

Who was this man Elihu, who spoke many words but was never addressed by Job, Eliphaz, Bildad, Zophar or God? Some have called this fourth speaker patronizing or self-important; others contend that he truly had Job's interest at heart.

Elihu has a longer genealogy than any other person in the book of Job. He was the son of Barachel the Buzite, of the family of Ram. As a Buzite, Elihu could have been related to Abraham, for Buz was a son of Nahor, Abraham's brother (Genesis 22:20-21). Evidently the Elihu of Job had been present during the long ash heap debate, silent and listening to Job pursue vindication from God. Or had he been present? Some scholars suggest the Elihu speeches were added later to the original book of Job because he was NOT referred to by Job, the three friends or by God. However, this study holds that Elihu's speeches were in the original for several reasons put forth by a second group of scholars. God may not have referred to Elihu when He called the three friends to account (42:7) because Elihu had spoken rightly about Him. Perhaps God chose not to speak to him for His own reasons as He chose not to answer Satan or Job's wife. Just as God did not choose to immediately answer Job's direct petitions (13:3, 15; 16:21, 30:20), He evidently chose not to directly answer Elihu.

Elihu provided an important transition to God's speeches.[1] When the older men fell silent, Elihu could wait no longer to speak. He declared himself full of words. He must "have relief" from his simmering thoughts and opinions. "Indeed my belly is like wine that has no vent; it is ready to burst like new wineskins" (32:20).

Chapter 32 records his initial speech. Elihu summarizes the previous thirty-one chapters in **32:2-3.** Write that summary below.

> **2-3**

> **2-3** What emotion did he express against Job and the three friends?

> **4-7** Why had Elihu contained his silence for so long?

> **10-13** Elihu declared that "age should speak and increased words should teach wisdom" (8). But he found such wisdom sorely lacking in the men of the dung hill debate (**11-12**). Instead, to whom did he advise Job to listen? **(10)**

> **21-22** What attitude did Elihu adopt toward Job and why?

In tomorrow's study, Elihu, full of words, challenges Job.

Day 2—Elihu: A Refuting Voice

Why do you complain against Him, that He does not give an account of all His doings?

—Job 33:13

Assignment: 1. Review Job chapters 34 and 35 and read selected passages.
2. Record in table 11.1 in today's study and in figures 0.2 through 0.4, the *Attributes of God* charts.

Do you identify with this young man's enthusiasm for God and his sense of bursting if not allowed to defend God? John Calvin wrote that Elihu cannot be blamed for "an exorbitant passion" for God.[2] Some commentators view Elihu as making no meaningful contribution, while others understand Elihu's role as one of preparing the way of the Lord.[3] Elihu may well hold the key to understanding the entire book of Job. What contribution <u>did</u> he make? Today we will look at how Elihu addressed Job's three major complaints.

It was finally Elihu's turn to challenge Job and defend God. Having listened intently to Job's complaints, he systematically dealt with each one. <u>Answer the questions below; then using numbers 1, 2 and 3 as guides, summarize your findings in table 11.1.</u>

1. Job's first major complaint against God according to Elihu in **33:8-11** and **34:5-6** was that God had treated him unjustly though Job was righteous. In response to that complaint, how did Elihu defend God's:

- omnipotence in **33:12**?

- justice in **34:10-12**?

- sovereignty in **34:13-15**?

- impartiality in **34:16-20**?

- omniscience in **34:21-25**?

- judgment of the wicked in **34:24-30**?

Knowing that an attack upon God's justice brought God's whole character into question, Elihu recalled everything he knew God to be. Fetching his knowledge from afar (36:3), he ascribed righteousness to his Maker.

Table 11.1 Job's Complaints and Elihu's Response

JOB'S COMPLAINTS AND ELIHU'S RESPONSE	
JOB'S COMPLAINTS	**ELIHU'S RESPONSE**
1. God's Justice	1.
2. God's Loftiness	2.
3. God's Silence	3.

2. Secondly, Job doubted that his righteousness was any advantage to God or any profit to himself (35:1-3). Elihu responded to Job's second complaint in **35:4-11**. How did Elihu affirm God's holiness and transcendence in **verse 7**?

How did Elihu affirm God's nearness and immanence in **verses 10 and 11**?

Elihu directed Job's attention to the heavens. "Look at the heavens and see; And behold the clouds—they are higher than you" (Job 35:5). In Job's oppression, he was inwardly focused and not looking for "God [his] Maker Who gives songs in the night." (35:10). Elihu wanted Job to realize that even though God is unaffected by our righteousness or by our wickedness, God does care about His people (35:10-11).

3. Job's third major complaint against God in 33:13 was that God was silent and did not give Job a reason for his suffering. What three reasons did Elihu give in **35:12-14** for Job's problem?

Elihu would have us check the motives and attitudes in our heart when our prayers are unanswered. You will learn more about prayer that pleases God on Day 4 of this lesson.

Might your prayers be hindered by any of the reasons identified above?

How like our all-sufficient God to challenge Job's faith with His seeming injustice, aloofness and silence. When He walked among men, our Savior Jesus Christ also dealt with people in a baffling manner. A Canaanite woman cried out to Him for mercy because her daughter was cruelly demon-possessed. Though she was not an Israelite, she called Him by the name of the promised Messiah, Son of David. Read **Matthew 15:22-28** to gain insight into Christ's purposeful use of silence. What was Christ's response to the Canaanite woman's cry for mercy?

Matthew 15:23

His disciples urged Christ to send her away because she was causing a disturbance. Christ replied that He was sent only to the lost sheep of the house of Israel. She, a Canaanite, was therefore excluded. Not deterred by His seeming aloofness, she bowed down before Him—the King James Version says that she worshiped him—and cried out, "Lord, help me!" Christ rebuffed her, stating, "It is not good to take the children's bread and throw it to the dogs" (15:26). The word Christ used for "dog" indicated a family pet. Therefore, it was not meant to be harsh. How did the Canaanite woman respond?

Matthew 15:27

What assessment did Christ make based on her response?

Matthew 15:28

What did Christ do for her?

Matthew 15:28

Knowing our Lord, we imagine that He spoke with a gleam in His eye, for He never spoke an idle word; rather, every word was purposeful. Christ was seemingly unfair, purposefully silent and aloof, all to elicit from her such great faith. We will in future studies understand that Job's experience was similar to that of this Canaanite woman. God's alleged injustice poured forth mercy. His seeming aloofness unfolded to reveal His care and accessibility. His silence yielded to a commendation of great faith.

Is there a circumstance in your life that seems unfair and about which God has been silent and aloof? How might Job's and the Canaanite woman's examples encourage your faith?

Day 3—Elihu: An Exhorting Voice

Then he will pray to God, and He will accept him.

—Job 33:26

Assignment: Read selected scripture.

Elihu had offered Job fresh perspectives on the spiritual benefit of suffering. He had taken Job to task over Job's complaints against God's treatment of him. He had also been quick to say that Job was impatient for God's answer. At this point, the reader of Elihu's many words may think, "Enough, Elihu!" But the young lecturer had not yet run out of words of advice and correction. Apparently, he considered himself satisfactorily competent and called to such an appointment. He also saw himself in a favorable position with God. In chapter 33:1-6, Elihu said that his words were from an upright heart and his lips spoke knowledge sincerely. "I am qualified to lecture you, Job, because I belong to God just as you do. God's Spirit has made me, and the breath of God gives me life. Refute me, Job, if you can."

1. Elihu's opinion of Job was similar to that of the three friends in that they all believed he had sinned and needed to repent. There was a major difference, however, in their views about exactly <u>when</u> and <u>how</u> Job sinned and <u>why</u> Job was to repent. The three friends pled with Job to repent of sins they claimed he committed <u>PRIOR</u> to his suffering and for which they believed he was being punished (11:11-19; 22:25-30). Elihu called for Job to repent of rash speech spoken against God <u>DURING</u> his suffering. How did Elihu describe Job in the verses below?

34:7

34:8

34:35

According to Elihu, what new charge in **34:37** was leveled against Job by "men of understanding" and "a wise man"?

Why?

What malediction did Elihu speak against Job in **34:36**?

Why?

Elihu's opinion of Job seems harsh until we realize Who Elihu was defending—the God of the universe! Elihu presented Job with a higher view of God and suggested that instead of complaining and questioning God, he needed to see God in his suffering and worship Him (33:24). We will see in chapters 38 through 42 that God challenged Job, who then repented of speaking about God without knowledge. God did not rebuke Elihu, leading us to conclude that Elihu spoke rightly about God.

> But Elihu is right to defend the justice of God, and he has advanced the discussion by suggesting that Job's greatest sin may not be something he said or did *before* the suffering started, but the rebellion he is displaying *in* the suffering.[4]

Would you be able to defend the God of the universe in such a way that He would approve?

On and on Elihu spoke, confident that Job could not refute what he had to say. "Job, you have been complaining against God because He doesn't give you an account of all His doings. Pray instead of complaining! If you pray instead, God will accept you. And what is more, Job, you are going to have to make some changes before God will hear you!"

2. What conditions for answered prayer did Elihu impose on Job?

33:27

35:12-13

37:24

Elihu minced no words. In his estimation, Job was sinning and perverting what was right, clinging to pride, impatient for a reply, being wise in his own eyes. Was Elihu correct about to whom God will and will not listen? Were the changes he confidently listed legitimate ones? Or were they products of skewed observation or youthful brashness?

3. Consider Elihu's contention that God does not listen to the prayers of a wicked man. Record your findings below then finish the summary statement in your own words.

Psalm 34:15

Proverbs 15:8

Proverbs 15:29

Isaiah 59:2

John 9:31

SUMMARY: God listens to

but God does not listen to

4. Job was not eligible for answered prayer according to Elihu. He called Job prideful, a man harboring sin, and thus a man whose cries fell on God's deaf ears. In His Word, God has made plain the truth that a believer's attitude influences the effectiveness of his prayers. Being a believer in Jesus Christ does not always give us unhindered access to God's throne. Look up the scriptures below and write the applicable hindrances to a believer's prayers. Complete the summary question.

Psalm 32:3-5

Psalm 66:18

James 4:3

SUMMARY: God will not listen to a believer's prayer if he

Basing your answer on the two summaries you have just written and what you have learned so far about Job, was Elihu correct in his assessment of to whom God listens? Why or why not?

Did Elihu's assessment apply to Job? Why or why not?

5. Does either condition that Elihu identified apply to your prayer today? We know from scripture that Christians are to examine themselves often, honestly probing their thoughts and motives, consciously putting off sin and perversion of what is right. We also know that we must confess sin for what it is, earnestly desiring fellowship and communion with God.

Wonderful guidance for prayer that honors God—and that God says He answers—is found in **1 John 3:22-24**, printed below. Meditate on the verses, considering each condition as you answer the questions.

> 22 and whatever we ask we receive from Him, because we keep His commandments and do the things that are pleasing in His sight. 23 This is His commandment, that we believe in the name of His Son Jesus Christ, and love one another, just as He commanded us. 24 The one who keeps His commandments abides in Him, and He in him. We know by this that He abides in us, by the Spirit whom He has given us.

What phrase spells out who has praying privileges with God? (**23**)

Only one who believes in His Son Jesus Christ, who is God-fearing and does His will, has the ear of God (John 9:30). The person who does not believe in Jesus Christ (the wicked man) has no praying privileges with Holy God.

The verb *to keep* in Greek means "to guard, to obey." Why does a Christian receive what he asks from God in the context of **verse 22**?

What does this say about obedience and answered prayer? See also **James 5:16**.

When we meet with God alone—if we want to ask of Him, if we want to receive from Him — we must come with an obedient heart. A Christian cannot expect any of the privileges due the Lord's child if he comes to Him in known disobedience, if he does not keep His commandments and do what is pleasing in His sight. Charles Spurgeon, the great British preacher of the nineteenth century, taught from the 1 John 3 passage that God's house is not run (accessed) by the disobedient. Spurgeon had wonderful counsel about the attitude God would have for His praying children:

God will not listen to His self-willed children, unless it is to hear them in anger and to answer them in wrath. Remember how He heard the prayer of Israel for flesh, and when the meat was yet in their mouths it became a curse to them (Num. 11:31-33). . . . We must have a childlike reverence of God, so that we feel, "Lord if what I ask for does not please You, neither would it please me. My desires are put into Your hands to be corrected. Strike the pen through every petition that I offer that is not right. And put in whatever I have omitted, even though I might not have desired it had I considered it. Good Lord, if I should have desired it, hear me as if I had desired it. . . . The Lord will be reverenced by those who are round about Him. They must have an eye to His pleasure in all that they do and ask, or He will not look upon them with favor. [5]

Are yours the fervent prayers of a righteous man (James 5:16)? Or are you disappointed in what seems to you a shallow prayer life?

Have you determined once and for all that you are in the faith? (See Lesson 10 Day 5.)

Are you obeying God's commandments as fully as you know how?

Elihu's conditions for answered prayer were: confess sin, remove pride and false motives and fear God. "Then he will pray to God, and He will accept him." Elihu continued by voicing a wonderful expectation for a believer of any era: "That he may see His face with joy, And He may restore His righteousness to man" (Job 33:26).

May we love and obey God so that we may experience the joy of true communion with Him, that we "will delight in the Almighty And lift up [our faces] to God" (Job 22:26).

Day 4—Elihu: A Teaching Voice

He opens the ears of men And seals their instruction . . . And commands that they return from evil. . . . He delivers the afflicted in their affliction, And opens their ear in time of oppression.

—Job 33:16; 36:10, 15

Assignment: 1. Review Job 33 and 36.
2. Record in figures 0.2 through 0.4, the *Attributes of God* charts.
3. Using figure 11.1, the *Interview Questionnaire* at the end of today's study, interview a woman whose life evidences a growing intimacy with the LORD because of trouble(s). Ask for permission to share her story with your discussion group.

After twenty-nine chapters of debate about why Job was suffering, Elihu offered a new perspective. He provided a vital bridge for Job between the monotonous views of the three friends and the authoritative voice of God which thundered from chapter 38 through chapter 42.

Elihu challenged Job's complaint that God "does not give an account of all His doings." He argued, "Indeed God speaks once, or twice, yet no one notices it" (Job 33:13-14). He detailed three ways God speaks to prepare a person's heart for a deeper relationship with Him or to prevent them from succumbing to temptation to sin.

1. First, God must cause a person to hear Him. What does God do?

33:16

God does this to prevent what three things?

33:17-18

Only by God's initiative can we hear the instruction of His Word. If a person like Job, of God-declared integrity, needed God's help in maintaining integrity, humility and steadfastness, how much more, then, do we need to ask God to open our ears to His Word.

Can you remember a time when God used His Word to prevent you from misconduct, pride or harm? Describe the process. What scripture did He use? Thank God for giving you ears to hear and a heart to obey so that further correction was not needed.

2. Second, when God opens a person's ears and seals his instruction, yet His warning is still not noticed, He may send others as His messengers to warn of the spiritual danger of a hardened heart. Elihu considered himself a messenger to Job, urging him, "Listen to me" (32:10; 33:1, 31, 33; 34:16). Elihu strongly exhorted Job in 33:12: "Behold, let me tell you, you are not right in this, for God is greater than man."

Have you experienced the benefit of God's messenger in the form of another Christian who exhorted you at a pivotal time, preventing sin or a hardened heart? Have you been such a messenger for others? Does your love for your Christian brothers and sisters include both the giving and the receiving of such concern and such action?

3. Third, if a person continues to neglect His word and ignore His messengers, God will increase His discipline through His providence, which may include suffering.

What is man chastened with, according to **33:19**?

What phrase did Elihu repeat in **33:18, 24, 28** and **30** to emphasize God's redemptive purpose for the chastening?

The pit was synonymous with Sheol, the place of the dead. According to Elihu, suffering from the hand of a loving and just God was corrective. It was meant to rescue a person from a condition worse than suffering, perhaps spiritual decline or physical death.

Elihu taught that the sufferer must recognize and act upon God's grace in opening his ear to instruction. What was the responsibility of the sufferer according to **36:10-11**?

With what result?

According to Elihu, if the sufferer disregarded the instruction, he would incur God's displeasure and judgment, resulting in heavier sorrows. If he did not repent, what would result?
36:12

Has the Lord used suffering to open your ears to instruction to keep you from further spiritual decline? Or are you presuming upon God's grace by refusing to hear and obey His instruction?

4. Elihu designated the unrepentant as hypocrites and contrasted them with the humble afflicted in **36:15**. What does God do for the afflicted in their affliction?

The MacArthur Study Bible suggests, "This was a new insight and perhaps, the most helpful thing Elihu said. He went beyond all that had been said about God's using suffering to chasten and bring repentance. He was saying that God used suffering to open men's ears, to draw them to Himself." [6]

Elihu asserted in 36:16 that God would have already brought Job out of distress if he had learned to trust Him for the spiritual freedom and feasts awaiting him. Once the lesson was learned, Job would be "enlightened with the light of life." That is, Job would experience restored health and fellowship with God (33:29-30). Thus, Elihu regarded suffering as instructive: "Behold, God is exalted in His power; Who is a teacher like Him?" (Job 36:22).

Recall a lesson Teacher God taught you through suffering. How were you "enlightened with the light of life"?

5. Bruce A. Ware, in *God's Greater Glory*, also considers suffering instructive. His five principles to understand suffering are listed below. The commentary on each and how the principles apply to Job are the authors'.

- *"Suffering is not, in itself, an* essential *good"* [8] Psalm 5:4 says of God, "For You are not a God who takes pleasure in wickedness; No evil dwells with you." This life is full of suffering and sadness and it is not right or good. Suffering hurts! We can be thankful that to be absent from the body is to be present with the Lord (2 Corinthians 5:8). For example, while rightfully grieving over the death of loved ones, we can be thankful that God will one day eradicate suffering: "He will wipe away every tear from their eyes; and there will no longer be any death; there will no longer be any mourning, or crying, or pain" (Revelation 21:4).

  Harm to Job from evil men with Satan as instigator was not good or right. Yet, though Job experienced excruciating grief, he believed that "Even after my skin is destroyed, Yet from my flesh I shall see God; Whom I myself shall behold, And whom my eyes will see and not another. My heart faints within me!" (Job 19:26-27).

- *"But suffering is ordained by God, and often it is intentionally used by God as an* instrumental *good"* [9] God may use suffering as a means of discipline and training. According to Hebrews 12:9-11, "We had earthly fathers to discipline us, and we respected them; shall we not much rather be subject to the Father of spirits, and live? For they disciplined us for a short time as seemed best to them, but He disciplines us for our good, so that we may share His holiness. All discipline for the moment seems not to be joyful, but sorrowful; yet to those who have been trained by it, afterwards it yields the peaceful fruit of righteousness."

  Job's devotion to God was tested by his suffering. He learned that nothing was more important than his relationship with God.

- *"God has promised His children that nothing befalls their lives that is not ordered and used by Him for their ultimate good."* [10] Romans 8:28 promises, "And we know that God causes all things to work together for good to those who love God, to those who are called according to His purpose."

God worked Job's suffering for good by revealing Himself to Job.

- *"God is more concerned with our character than with our comfort, with our transformation than with the trials necessary to get us where He wants us to be"* [11] Romans 5:3-5 reminds us to "exult in our tribulations, knowing that tribulation brings about perseverance; and perseverance, proven character; and proven character, hope; and hope does not disappoint, because the love of God has been poured out within our hearts through the Holy Spirit who was given to us." We are to "consider it all joy, my brethren, when you encounter various trials, knowing that the testing of your faith produces endurance. And let endurance have its perfect result, so that you may be perfect and complete, lacking in nothing" (James 1:2-4).

As all of the relationships and comforts of his life were stripped away, Job's character was being transformed. He finally saw himself as insignificant and God as sovereign.

- *"Accepting the divine purpose for suffering does not require a passive acquiescence to suffering."* [12] We can pray for healing and deliverance. Paul did in 2 Corinthians 12:7-10: "There was given me a thorn in the flesh, a messenger of Satan to torment me—to keep me from exalting myself! Concerning this I implored the Lord three times that it might leave me. And He has said to me, 'My grace is sufficient for you, for power is perfected in weakness.' Most gladly, therefore, I will rather boast about my weaknesses, so that the power of Christ may dwell in me. Therefore I am well content with weakness, with insults, with distresses, with persecutions, with difficulties, for Christ's sake; for when I am weak, the I am strong."

Job sought understanding and relief and ultimately received it.

Think of an instance of suffering in your own life. How might you use the above principles to interpret your suffering biblically?

Elihu understood Job's suffering as an ear-opening opportunity to know God better and as a measure of the Lord's providential care and lovingkindness (37:13). And indeed, Job's silence during Elihu's speeches may indicate that he was listening.

Do you have a sense of anticipation, an eagerness to have the LORD open your ears as He did for Job when He finally answered him out of the whirlwind?

Remember to record any meaningful insights in figures 0.2 through 0.4, the *Attributes of God* charts.

Interview Questionnaire

You have journeyed with Job through his trials and his triumph in the LORD. This is a journey that others have taken and who, like Job, see the LORD afresh. They delight in crediting the LORD for His faithfulness and goodness. Choose a woman whose life evidences a growing intimacy with the LORD because of troubles. Plan a time to interview her. You will be blessed by spending time with her as you conduct this interview. Remember to ask her permission to share her testimony with the group.

1. What was your relationship with the LORD like before the trouble?

2. What were the circumstances of the trouble?

3. What was your initial reaction?

4. What were your immediate needs?

5. How were those needs met?

Figure 11.1 Interview questionnaire for woman who knows the Lord more deeply through troubles

Figure 11.1 Interview questionnaire continued

6. Describe the point at which you began to "see" God more clearly.

7. What scripture was especially meaningful to you?

8. What truth about God did you learn that you can share with others now?

For the Interviewer:

After the interview, answer the following questions and be prepared to share your answers with the discussion group.

1. Did you find out anything surprising during the interview?

2. What response did you have to the information?

3. What was most meaningful to you about the interview?

4. After hearing all that your interviewee went through to get to know God better, would you be willing to pray the following adaptation of Ephesians 3:19, John 1:16 and Colossians 1:19, even if the prayer could be fulfilled only through experiencing troubles?

"May I experience every part of You that is possible this side of heaven—the love of Christ, the fullness of God in Christ."

Day 5—Elihu: An Exalting Voice

Listen to this, O Job, stand and consider the wonders of God...the wonders of [O]ne perfect in knowledge.

—Job 37:14, 16

Assignment: 1. If the weather permits, do this lesson sitting outside. If not, sit beside a window with a view of nature.
2. Read Job 36:22—37, printed in this lesson, and consider the wonders of God.
3. Record in figures 0.2 through 0.4, the *Attributes of God* charts.

The highest drama of Elihu's speech occurred when he instructed Job to listen, stand and consider God's wonders. Robert L. Alden deemed it "ultimately the solution to his problem and the cure for his ills, physical, emotional, and attitudinal."[13] It was also God's means to prepare Job for a direct encounter with Himself. Already, Elihu's speeches had corrected Job's distorted views of God and had given Job a more palatable view of his sufferings. Just as God had opened Job's ears to instruction, He would also open Job's eyes to His majesty. And we are blessed to join Job on this eye-opening, heart-trembling excursion into God's creation. We listen as Elihu focuses on the weather phenomenon to demonstrate the contrast between God's power and perfect knowledge, and man's limited power and knowledge. (In Lesson 12, Creator God Himself will continue the demonstration with a guided tour through His animal kingdom.) <u>As you read **Job 36:22-33 and 37:1-24**, make a list in the right margin of the elements of weather mentioned.</u>

Job 36	Elements
[22] Behold, God is exalted in His power; Who is a teacher like Him? [23] Who has appointed Him His way, And who has said, 'You have done wrong'? [24] Remember that you should exalt His work, Of which men have sung.	

Pause to exalt God's work and sing to Creator God.

	Elements
[25] All men have seen it; Man beholds from afar. [26] Behold, God is exalted, and we do not know Him; The number of His years is unsearchable. [27] For He draws up the drops of water,	

They distill rain from the mist,

²⁸ Which the clouds pour down,   **Elements**

They drip upon man abundantly.

²⁹ Can anyone understand the spreading of the clouds,

  The thundering of His pavilion?

    Look at the clouds. Are they puffy cumulus clouds? Layered stratus clouds? High wispy cirrus clouds? Or are you near mountains to observe lenticular clouds hovering at the peaks?

Peek ahead at **37:12-13** to find out God's purposes in the "spreading of the clouds."

                                                    Elements

³⁰ Behold, He spreads His lightning about Him,

And He covers the depths of the sea.

³¹ For by these He judges peoples;

He gives food in abundance.

³² He covers His hands with the lightning,

And commands it to strike the mark.

³³ Its noise declares His presence;

The cattle also, concerning what is coming up.

    What <u>is</u> coming up? The lightning and thunder declare His presence! God is preparing us for when He speaks in chapters 38 through 41. In addition to listing the weather elements, <u>circle references and descriptions of God's voice in **37:1-8**</u>.

Job 37   **Elements**

¹ At this also my heart trembles, And leaps from its place.

² Listen closely to the thunder of His voice,

And the rumbling that goes out from His mouth.

³ Under the whole heaven He lets it loose,

And His lightning to the ends of the earth.

⁴ After it, a voice roars; He thunders with His majestic voice,

And He does not restrain the lightnings when His voice is heard.

⁵ God thunders with His voice wondrously,

Doing great things which we cannot comprehend.

⁶ For to the snow He says, 'Fall on the earth,'

Elements

And to the downpour and the rain, 'Be strong.'

[7] He seals the hand of every man,

That all men may know His work.

[8] Then the beast goes into its lair And remains in its den.

There is no escape from God's works. What happens to the activity of man and beast at the time of a downpour?

37:7-8

Elements

[9] Out of the south comes the storm,

And out of the north the cold.

[10] From the breath of God ice is made,

And the expanse of the waters is frozen.

[11] Also with moisture He loads the thick cloud;

He disperses the cloud of His lightning.

[12] It changes direction, turning around by His guidance,

That it may do whatever He commands it

On the face of the inhabited earth.

[13] Whether for correction, or for His world,

Or for lovingkindness, He causes it to happen.

What control does God exert over every little cloud and every big storm?

37:11-12

Where does He cause it to happen?

37:12

Why does He cause it to happen?

37:13

What kinds of questions surface because "He causes it to happen"? Are you unsettled by the thought that the storms of life are "turning around by His guidance, that they may do whatever He commands"?

In 37:14-20, Elihu asked a series of rhetorical questions, a technique God also employed with his eighty scientific questions in chapters 38 through 41. Perhaps the Spirit of God inspired Elihu to use this devise as yet another means of preparing Job for the intense grilling he would soon receive from God. The questions also emphasize the contrast between no-knowledge, no-power Job and perfect-knowledge, all-powerful God. <u>Circle examples of God's superiority. Underline the phrases that indicate man's inferiority.</u>

Elements

¹⁴ Listen to this, O Job,
Stand and consider the wonders of God.
¹⁵ Do you know how God establishes them,
And makes the lightning of His cloud to shine?
¹⁶ Do you know about the layers of the thick clouds,
The wonders of one perfect in knowledge,
¹⁷ You whose garments are hot,
When the land is still because of the south wind?
¹⁸ Can you, with Him, spread out the skies,
Strong as a molten mirror?
¹⁹ Teach us what we shall say to Him;
We cannot arrange our case because of darkness.
²⁰ Shall it be told Him that I would speak?
Or should a man say that he would be swallowed up?

Look up at the clouds and ponder **37:16**. What could the layers of thick clouds symbolize about God?

Elements

²¹ Now men do not see the light which is bright in the skies;
But the wind has passed and cleared them.
²² Out of the north comes golden splendor;
Around God is awesome majesty.
²³ The Almighty—we cannot find Him;
He is exalted in power
And He will not do violence to justice and abundant righteousness.
²⁴ Therefore men fear Him;
He does not regard any who are wise of heart.

Notice the darkness/light motif in 37:18-21. Comparing the skies to a metal mirror whose existence is a mystery to us, Elihu bemoaned that in our darkness or lack of knowledge we do not know how to approach the One perfect in knowledge. "For now we see in a mirror dimly…" (1

Corinthians 13:12). Just as the wind passes by and clears the skies, so the Holy Spirit must pass by to clear our hearts and to prepare us for God's presence.

Meditate upon the theology of 37:23, the hiddenness of the Almighty, the all-sufficient God. We cannot find Him, yet He is seen and understood in His power over creation, His justice and His righteousness.

In his final words, Elihu cautioned of the blinding brightness of God's glory that one would encounter when attempting to approach awesome, majestic God. Even to speak would risk being swallowed up. He reminded Job how to approach holy God – with reverential fear. Though Elihu's teaching on the spiritual benefit of suffering was helpful, human knowledge was found lacking. God has the final word and "does not regard any who are wise of heart." Elihu ended with a call for his listeners to confess our human limitations and submit, bow down, pay homage to and reverence almighty God.

Spend the rest of your study time looking up at the clouds and bowing down to the One perfect in knowledge and mighty in strength.

Remember to record any meaningful insights in figures 0.2 through 0.4, the *Attributes of God* charts.

REFLECTIONS ON LESSON 11

Truths I have learned that deepen my relationship with the Lord

Day 1

Describe the scene at the time of Elihu's entrance into the discussion.

How did Elihu exhibit respect for his elders?

What is one way to enter an already-existing discussion?

What is your opinion of Elihu? What did he contribute to your understanding of Job's situation?

Day 2

Defend God's justice, loftiness and silence.

Which is easy to defend? Which is difficult to defend? Why do you think that is?

Day 3

What is the criteria for effective praying in **1 John 3:22-24**?

Do you have any "unanswered" prayers? If so, evaluate yourself and your prayers based upon the biblical teachings of Day 3.

What are some reasons God answers, "No"?

Day 4

How did Elihu's teaching on suffering differ from that of the three friends?

Elihu showed Job what alternative way to view his suffering?

What benefit has suffering been to you?

How has your interview impacted your prayer life?

Share your interview experience from figure 11.1 with your discussion group.

Day 5

List three ways that Elihu helped Job to hear from God.

Give at least one way that Elihu prepared you to hear from God.

Notes

1. Roy B. Zuck, *JOB* (Chicago: Moody, 1978. Copyright 1978 by Moody Bible Institute of Chicago), 140-42.

2. John Calvin, *Sermons from Job* (Grand Rapids: Baker, 1990. Copyright 1952 by Wm. B. Eerdmans Publishing), 220.

3. Zuck, 141, 162.

4. D. A. Carson, *How Long, O Lord?* (Grand Rapids: Baker, 1990. Copyright 1990, 2006 by D. A. Carson), 149-50.

5. Charles Spurgeon, *The Power of Prayer in a Believer's Life* (Lynnwood: Emerald, 1993. Copyright 1993 by Lance C. Wubbells), 109-10.

6. John MacArthur, *The MacArthur Study Bible* (Nashville: Word, 1997. Copyright 1997 by Word), 733.

7. Bruce A.Ware, *God's Greater Glory* (Wheaton IL: Crossway, 2004. Copyright 2004 by Bruce A. Ware), 164-75.

8. Ware, 165.

9. Ware, 167.

10. Ware, 171.

11. Ware, 173.

12. Ware, 175.

13. Robert L. Alden, *The New American Commentary: Job* (Nashville: Broadman and Holman, 1993. Copyright 1993 by Broadman and Holman), 362.

```
┌─────────────────────────────────────────────┐
│                                               │
│            LESSON 12                          │
│                                               │
│     GOD SPEAKS! JOB ANSWERS                   │
│                                               │
└─────────────────────────────────────────────┘
```

Day 1—God Speaks! Job Answers: (Part 1)

Then the LORD answered Job out of the whirlwind and said, 'Who is this that darkens counsel By words without knowledge?'

—Job 38:1, 2

Assignment: 1. Read chapters 38, 39 and 40:1-5 carefully. Notice the format and the beautiful imagery that are befitting the all-powerful Lord of creation. Because this study does not examine the imagery in detail, you will want to do so in your first reading.

2. Record in figures 0.2 through 0.4, the *Attributes of God* charts.

At last! The Lord speaks!! But...what is this He is saying?
Foundations of the earth?
Morning stars singing?
A sea with doors?
Recesses of the deep?
Storehouses of the hail?
Rain in a desert?
Ordinances of heavens?
Tipping water jars?
Mountain goats and wild donkeys and wild oxen?
An oaf of an ostrich?
A majestic war horse?
An espying eagle?

What IS this that the LORD is saying?

Surprise, Job! You have been waiting and waiting and demanding in a forlorn and quarrelsome manner that God speak to you, that God answer you, that God show up and make Himself known to you. Well, here He is, Job. And it is evident from this powerful, dark, swirling wind that He isn't messing around with pleasantries.

> Who is this that darkens counsel By words without knowledge? Now gird up your loins like a man, And I will ask you, and you instruct me!
>
> —Job 38:2, 3

Yes, Job, you are about to hear wondrous and unexpected words from the almighty, all-sufficient God. Not words that will answer the questions that you so boldly asked but words that will shame yet comfort you, words that will correct yet reconcile you with your God. Now, be still and listen.

Prior to faithfully pursuing this study on Job, had you been one of those Bible readers who dutifully slugged through the book but really enjoyed only three chapters, the first two and the last? Or perhaps you have lingered appreciatively over God's speeches in chapters 38 through 41. If you are among the latter, you are in good company. God's answer to Job is the best-known portion of the book.

Elihu had just finished instructing Job about God's might in a storm and of God's thundering voice when God spoke out of the whirlwind. In the Old Testament, an appearance of God, called a *theophany*, was often set in a whirlwind or storm to emphasize the awesomeness of the occasion. Thunder and lighting and thick clouds accompanied the LORD when He came down upon Mount Sinai to speak to Moses and the Israelites (Exodus 19:16, 20). But this time, God spoke only to Job and directly to him. Job did not hide his face or seem to fear the awesome voice in the whirlwind. He did not beg for an intermediary to record God's message as the Israelites did Moses. Instead, he remained silent, listening, speaking only twice.

That the LORD finally spoke is surprising, and what he says—and doesn't say—is unexpected.

> It is typical of the attitude of the Bible that God's questions virtually restrict themselves to this world, in which man was placed as God's vice-regent (Gen. 1:28, Psa. 8:6). God scarcely asks Job about the mysteries of the stars on their silent way, but He faces him with everyday things of this world, in which man is ever tempted to speak Himself [sic. "himself"] free of his Creator.[1]

1. Job had been presumptuous and impetuous in his dealings with the LORD. Prior to God's speaking, Job had demanded certain actions from Him. Look up **Job 31:35**. What request,

summarized in this verse, had Job repeatedly made?

Job was prepared to answer the charges of a bill of indictment. He wanted his day in court. However, if for some reason God did not provide that opportunity, Job expected God the Judge to issue a verdict. What verdict did Job expect? (You know the answer to this question from your study.)

The LORD began his thundering interrogation with this simple question and command: "Where were you when I laid the foundation of the earth? Tell me if you have understanding." The unexpected followed! Refer to your assigned reading for today to catalogue a portion of God's surprising answer.

Did God issue a bill of indictment?

Did God pronounce a verdict?

What, if anything, did God say about Eliphaz's, Zophar's and Bildad's accusation that God had abandoned Job because he had sinned?

How did God answer Job's pleas to know why he was suffering?

How did God fulfill Job's wish for an advocate or witness who would stand up for him?

How would you summarize God's answer?

2. God's defense was definitely not what Job expected. He was anticipating the confrontation that he had called for in 9:35 and 13:22. From the whirlwind, God upended those expectations. "Who is this that darkens counsel by words without knowledge? Now gird up your loins like a man and I will ask you, and you instruct me!" Job the plaintiff was now Job the defendant! God called on Job to stand up like a man and act like one.

Yet God's counter-questioning was not meant to test Job's knowledge of the world around him. God's counter-questioning was not meant to humiliate Job nor to force him to confess that his claim to be in the right was false. God's counter-questioning was not meant to rebuke Job for questioning God.

On the contrary the highest nobility of every person is to be thus enrolled by God Himself in His school of Wisdom. And the schoolroom is the world! For Job the exciting discoveries to which God leads him bring a giant advance in knowledge, knowledge of himself and of God, for the two always go together in the Bible.[2]

Job gained knowledge about himself and about God as he listened silently to his Maker. It is significant to Job's relationship with God that, beginning in chapter 38, God is called Yahweh, not *El Shaddai* as in chapters 3 through 37. God used His personal covenant name Yahweh (LORD) in the prologue to signal his personal relationship with Job. But Job, the three friends and Elihu called God *El Shaddai*, God the Almighty, which in the book of Job reflects a more distant, detached God.[3]

Table 12.1 is designed to help you understand God's counter-questioning of Job. It is divided into three parts: questions, references and the message. You are given the references and God's message. As you scan the references for pertinent questions, choose from among them any questions that will help you remember God's message. Keep in mind God's personal relationship with his servant Job.

Table 12.1 God's Message

GOD'S MESSAGE		
QUESTIONS	REFERENCE	GOD'S MESSAGE
	38:4-7	I created the world. You were not present when I did so. You are ignorant of things you cannot see.
	38:8-38	I control the weather. I command the constellations. I rule over the ordinances of heaven. You do not.
	38:39-39:30	I made and control the creatures of earth. You have no power like mine to understand the workings of the natural realm.

What in God's messages surprised you?

What in God's messages elevated your view of Him?

> Then the Lord said to Job, 'Will the faultfinder contend with the Almighty? Let him who reproves God answer it.'
>
> —Job 40:1, 2

3. God's first speeches began with a challenge (38:2, 3) and ended with one (40:1, 2). The noun *faultfinder* occurs only here in the Old Testament and comes from a common verb meaning "to admonish or correct." Job had contended with God at least twice about bringing a court case against Him (10:2; 23:6), but now God called Job into account. How could Job present an indictment against God? He knew little about God's ways and power over nature; how could he expect God to answer to him?

Job had been silent while the almighty God spoke. Now he was challenged to reply: "Behold, I am insignificant; what can I reply to You? I lay my hand on my mouth. Once I have spoken, and I will not answer; even twice, and I will add nothing more" (**Job 40:3-5**). What change can you see in Job's response?

What brought about this change?

Job's attitude moved from haughty, self-confidence (13:22), demanding that God answer him, to admitting that beside God, he was nothing. Instead of repeating his boast that he would approach God like a prince (31:37), he was reduced to humility with nothing to say. No longer did he entertain thoughts of reproving or arguing with God (13:3, 15). In a gesture he had recommended for his counselors (21:5), Job placed his hand on his mouth.

Alas, Job did not admit any wrong speaking. He admitted speaking unnecessarily and to repeating himself. The LORD continued to speak. In tomorrow's study, you will find that under God's probing, Job entered into a tender relationship with his LORD.

Day 2—God Speaks! Job Answers: (Part 2)

Then the LORD answered Job out of the storm and said, 'Now gird up your loins like a man; I will ask you, and you instruct Me. Will you really annul My judgment?'

— Job 40:6-8

Assignment: Read Job 40:6 through 42:6.

Prepare again to hear your LORD, Job!

Don't be surprised if He continues to remain silent about your suffering.

Don't be surprised if He continues to offer no explanation of His actions.

Don't be surprised if He continues to deny you a courtroom session.

The LORD had more to teach Job about Himself. He launched a second round of questioning out of the storm (whirlwind). God's second speech followed the same pattern as the first, a quick succession of challenging questions ending with a reply from Job.

Keep in mind Job's circumstances as his listened to the LORD. Once again picture him on the dung heap scraping his blackening and rotting skin, a scorned man bereft of all family, possessions and honor, smarting under the misunderstanding of his friends and the correction of young Elihu. He had nothing; in the eyes of his world, he was nothing.

1. God had already impressed upon Job that he was woefully lacking in adequate knowledge of God's control over His creation. With His very first question in the second round, God challenged Job's accusations that He had been unjust in His rule of the world.

"Will you really annul My judgment?"

"Will you condemn Me that you may be justified?"

Job had been so intent on defending his own integrity that he had ended up blaming God.

What had he said? Review his complaints by listing them from the scriptures below.

6:29

9:20

9:24

13:18

27:2

Elihu, the fourth advisor, had warned Job about the error of his charges against God. From the scriptures below, list a few of Job's charges against God that Elihu had itemized.

33:10-11

33:13

34:31-33

35:2-3

36:23

2. If Job's justice or righteousness were truly superior to God's, then his power to execute that justice over men and world affairs would also be superior to God's. What single question did God ask that eliminated that possibility?

40:9

Of course the answer is "no!" Not only is Job a mere man with a mere man's sense of justice; he possesses only a mere man's power to enforce that justice. He does not have a voice of thunder, much less "an arm like God," the biblical metaphor for strength.

3. Next, the LORD commanded Job, a wretched, dishonored and diseased man, "Adorn yourself with eminence and dignity, And clothe yourself with honor and majesty" (40:10). What descriptions of God are common to the following verses?

Psalm 93:1

Psalm 96:6

Psalm 104:1

"Job," the LORD said, "if you want to rule in strength as I do over the affairs of men, you must do so in eminence and majesty." And Job, while you are ruling in honor and majesty over the affairs of men, "Pour out the overflowings of your anger, And look on everyone who is proud, and make him low. Look on everyone who is proud, and humble him, And tread down the wicked where they stand. Hide them in the dust together; Bind them in the hidden place. Then I also will confess to you, That your own right hand can save you" (40:11-14). You have been asking for proof of My justice, Job. Bring down the wicked as I can. Humble the proud. Take on responsibility for the death of the wicked. You do these things and you will convince me that you can save yourself.

4. The LORD had dealt graciously with Job. He patiently demonstrated His legitimate right to rule by giving him examples from nature that Job could understand. Now the LORD'S speech ascends to crescendo as He leads Job past his first confession of "know-nothing" (40:3-5) to humble confession of God's power and His justice over the affairs of men.

The LORD established his dominance as Creator-Maker by using two more animals as examples. He chose to exhibit Behemoth and Leviathan, creatures that have come to symbolize something invincible and untamable in modern language.

Behemoth, the most terrifying land animal, was chief of the works of God (40:19). Only God, his Maker, could dominate him.

How did God put Job in his right, lowly place with the example of Behemoth?

40:15

God reserved the fiercest creature to firmly illustrate His ownership of the universe (41:1-34). God's long description of Leviathan takes up one-fourth of His speeches. The invincible Leviathan could not be domesticated. No man could pierce Leviathan's hide or jaw with a fishhook. The mere sight of the fierce aquatic beast made a courageous man weak. If a man dared creep close enough to touch the beast, he would not do it again.

What thunderous comparison did the LORD God, Owner of the universe, make regarding the power and authority of Leviathan and Himself?

41:10-11

If the man Job could not face down Leviathan, how could he challenge God, the beast's Maker?

"Who then is he that can stand before Me?" (41:10).

No one can stand before God on his own merit and strength.

Figure 12.1 provides a summary of Job's confession in an unexpected form. Let this unusual presentation give you a more profound understanding of the nature of Job's repentance.

SPECIAL EDITION

Uz Chronicle

UZ'S FINEST NEWSPAPER

PRINTED NEAR THE CITY GATE   AT THE TIME OF JOB   1 PAGE   1 EDITION   3 FIGS

God extracts confession
Local dung hill resident repents in dust and ashes

By Special Report
Uz Chronicle

Then Job answered the Lord and said, "I know that You can do all things, And that no purpose of Yours can be thwarted. '*Who is this that hides counsel without knowledge?*'

Therefore, I have declared that which I did not understand, Things too wonderful for me, which I did not know. '*Hear, now and I will speak; I will ask You and You will instruct me.*'

I have heard of You by hearing of the ear, but now my eye sees You; therefore I retract, And I repent in dust and ashes."

—Job 42:1-6
(Emphasis added.)

Job acknowledges lowly position

Job, former wealthy UZ landowner, backed down yesterday from his view that an unjust God had ignored him. Job, convinced he cannot stand before God, admitted that he cannot rule the world and has no power to execute justice like God does. He also gave up the notion that he has eminence to govern men and power to bring down the wicked.

INSIDE: Page 7

3 friends indicted for wrong-speaking
Job drafted to intercede
No mention of exuberant young counselor

Figure 12.1. Newspaper headline: God extracts confession

Day 3—The Lord Restores Job

"I will accept Job because he has spoken of me what is right!" . . . The LORD restored the fortunes of Job when he prayed for his friends, and the LORD increased all that Job had two-fold.

—Job 42:8 (paraphrased), 10

Assignment: Read Job 42.

In yesterday's edition of the Uz Chronicle, you read the distinction Job made between having heard of God in the past and seeing Him in the present. He had a devotion to the LORD that was untested. His "seeing" symbolized an intimacy with the powerful, purposeful and providential God. God's questioning of Job had done its work. It had its intended effect to quicken his conscience to God's presence and to assure him that God was not against him but FOR him.

When Job sees the LORD in his new intimacy, what does he "see"?

- You can do all things.

- Your purposes cannot be thwarted.

- You are incomprehensible.

1. In 42:3, Job agreed with God that what he had said about Him prior to his confession was wrong. Job's confession implied that he had darkened counsel (38:2), found fault with and reproved God (40:2), and questioned His justice (40:8).

The reason Job quoted God in 42:3 and 4 was to emphasize his agreement with God that he had spoken without knowledge. "Therefore, I repent." Job did not repent of some specific sins from the past of which his friends had accused him. Rather, he repented of what God had charged against him. He changed his mind and despised and rejected the earlier remarks he had made about God.

Only the LORD could elicit such a confession from Job and bring about a change of mind. The erroneous, argumentative efforts of his three friends to set him straight failed. But God and His Word have the power to deepen a man's true knowledge of His wise ways.

Has there been a time in your life when you have "seen" God afresh? Describe it.

What change did that elicit in your life?

How did that change affect your witness to others of God's power?

2. A reader of Job doesn't know at what point in the theophany the three friends and Elihu were present. We do not know for how much of the LORD's speeches, if any, they were present. But we do know that after Job's confession, the LORD spoke directly to Eliphaz. Write below the LORD's words in **42:7**.

3. God's rebuke set in motion a series of reversals. First, the LORD vindicated Job and rebuked Eliphaz, Bildad and Zophar. They had been Job's accusers, yet they were now the accused! Why? God said that they did not speak rightly about Him. They claimed that God was punishing Job for some specific sin. With this allegation, they presumed to speak for God. They had characterized God as being too high and holy to care about Job. As you learned in Lesson 11, it is unknown why God did not include Elihu in his rebuke.

4. In another reversal, God reinstated his servant Job as priest (Job 1:5) and drafted him to intercede for the three friends. What did the LORD instruct Eliphaz to do?

Notice that the men offered their own sacrifices. Remember that the Mosaic Law's sacrificial system had not yet been instated, but the number and kinds of animals God ordered were in line with the common practice of that ancient day. The large amount of burnt offerings may indicate the seriousness of the offense. More significant than the kind of sacrifice is God's mercy to allow the friends to atone for their "folly." What did the LORD instruct Job to do?

Eliphaz, Bildad and Zophar needed restoration as much as Job—they just didn't know it! When Job in his role of priest prayed for them, what did God say he WOULD and WOULD NOT do? **42:8**

After they all had done as the LORD told them, the LORD accepted Job. The literal Hebrew means that the LORD "lifted up the face of" Job. Job finally experienced the ultimate comfort he had been seeking.

Only a short time earlier, Job had longed for a mediator "to lay hands on us both" (Job 9:33). Now God was calling upon Job to mediate between Himself and the three friends. God taught us through His dealings with Eliphaz that we should not attempt to approach the presence of God in our name or upon our own merit. God did not accept Eliphaz's approach but insisted upon Job's intercession. We, too, need a mediator/intercessor. In this respect, when Job interceded for his friends, he foreshadowed Jesus Christ, "the one Mediator also between God and men" (1 Timothy 2:5).

5. Finally, Job experienced a positive reversal of fortune. The Lord graciously doubled Job's original fortune and blessed his latter days more than his beginning (42:10, 12). God did not double the number of Job's children, but he replaced the first set of seven sons and three daughters with another set of seven sons and three daughters. In an uncustomary provision, Job shared his inheritance with his beautiful daughters as well as with his sons. For the rest of his long life, Job enjoyed his children and grandchildren and great-grandchildren.

Please rejoice with Job and write out the special celebration invitation in figure 12.2.

Come Celebrate
the LORD's Restoration of Job

With whom:

Where:

Be ready to:

Bring:

Rejoice with us that the LORD has doubled Job's fortune with

Livestock

_____

_____

_____

_____

Children:

_____

_____

The LORD gave, the LORD took away and the LORD has given again!

Blessed be the name of the LORD!

Figure 12.2. Invitation to Job's celebration

Day 4—The LORD of Job's Beginning and Latter Days

The LORD blessed the latter days of Job more than his beginning.
—Job 42:12

Assignment: Read Job 1, 2 and 42.

That the LORD would bless Job in his beginning and bless him again in his latter days demonstrates God's grace and sovereignty as Job had so eloquently extolled in 1:21: "The LORD gave and the LORD has taken away. Blessed be the name of the LORD." In His wisdom and by His gracious compassion and tender mercy, God chooses whom He will bless, when He will bless, and how He will bless. Jesus reminded us in Luke 12:31-32 (KJV) to seek first God and His kingdom, for "It is your Father's good pleasure to give you the kingdom."

The following questions are designed to help you compare and contrast the beginning of Job with his latter days. Read **Job chapters 1, 2** and **42** and write your answers to the questions in table 12.2.

1. Where did the feasts take place in **1:4** and **42:11**?

2. What function did Job perform in **1:5** and **42:8-10**?

3. Compare Job's prosperity in **1:2-3** and **42:8-10**.

4. What details do you find about Job's last three daughters in **42:14-15**?

5. How was Job commended by God in **1:8, 2:3** and **42:7-8**?

6. What did God call Job in **1:8** and **2:3**, as well as four times in **chapter 42**?

7. What did Satan allege about Job's motive for worshiping God in **1:9** and **2:4-5**? When did Job repent and worship God, before or after his restoration (**42:1-6**)?

8. What did Job know about the heavenly council of **chapter one** at that time? In his latter day?

9. What did Job know about the reason he was suffering?

10. What did the author of the book of Job reveal to the reader about the source of Job's suffering, according to **1:12, 2:6** and **42:11**?

11. How was Job different in **chapter 42**, according to **verse 6**?

12. What does **42:17** say about Job's length of days? If Job was around the age of 70 in chapter one, how old would he have been at the time of his death?

Table 12.2 Comparison and contrast of Job's beginning and latter days

COMPARISON AND CONTRAST OF JOB'S BEGINNING AND LATTER DAYS	
THE BEGINNING OF JOB	THE LATTER DAYS OF JOB
1.	
2	
3.	
4.	
5.	
6.	
7.	
8.	
9.	
10.	
11.	
12.	

In the beginning of the book of Job, the feasting mentioned took place in the house of each of Job's sons. The feasting in chapter 42 took place in Job's house. Because he had no children at the time of his restoration, he celebrated with his brothers, sisters and acquaintances who knew him before his suffering. It is unknown whether the Mrs. Job of chapter 1, not mentioned in chapter 42, is the mother of the second set of children. While details were not given about Job's first three daughters, chapter 42 describes his last three daughters as the most beautiful women in all the land. Their names, Jemimah, meaning "dove," Keziah, meaning "perfume," and Keran-happuch, meaning "horn of eye paint," or in modern terminology "bottle of eye make-up," all emphasized their beauty.[5] Such details reinforce the idea of Job's restored fortune, as beauty was an ancient symbol of wealth. Job made his daughters heiresses with their brothers, unusual for that culture, signifying that Job was reestablished as the "greatest of all the men of the east" (Job 1:3).

Though the heavenly council of chapter one was not mentioned in chapter 42, the author interpreted Job's suffering by declaring in 42:11 that all who attended the feast "consoled him and comforted him for all the evil the LORD had brought on him." Having described the unforgettable scene of the heavenly council in chapter one in which the LORD gave Satan permission to test Job, the author later in chapter 42 attributed Job's suffering to the LORD. John Piper wrote that Job was not comforted by focusing upon such secondary causes of his suffering as the Sabean raiders or the Chaldean marauders. When Job recognized God as the first cause and submitted to His providence, he gained true comfort[6] and was able to express:

> The LORD gave and the LORD has taken away. Blessed be the name of the LORD.
> —Job 1:21

> Shall we indeed accept good from God and not accept adversity?
> —Job 2:10

> I know that You can do all things, And that no purpose of Yours can be thwarted.
> —Job 42:2

When Job's devotion to the LORD was tested, his cry was "Wherefore, I abhor myself and repent in dust and ashes" (42:6, KJV). Job's circumstances had not changed, but he had. He knew the LORD afresh. In worshiping the LORD without any expectation that he would receive anything in return, he disproved Satan's allegation that he worshiped God only for material gain. The LORD of Job's beginning and latter days is truly "full of compassion and is merciful" (James 5:11) and worthy of true worship.

How will you endure so that you may know that the Lord is full of compassion and is merciful?

Day 5—Knowing the Lord More Deeply

I have heard of You by the hearing of the ear; But now my eye sees You.

—Job 42:5

Assignment: Review figures 0.2 through 0.4, the *Attributes of God* charts.

Today concludes your study. Congratulations for faithfully completing *Our ALL-SUFFICIENT GOD: Beyond Suffering in the Book of Job*! Are you not grateful and overwhelmed at how God has revealed Himself to you through His dealings with Job? You have meditated on the grandeur of our incomprehensible God. You have seen that God does great and unsearchable things and is Creator of and Judge over all the earth. He is the One who is able to save and to destroy. In His power and providence, He is merciful and kind. God does what His soul desires.

This study was designed to help you know more intimately your all-sufficient God and to speak rightly about Him. Using figures 0.2 through 0.4, the *Attributes of God* charts, as a reminder of what you have learned, consider the following questions.

- o Do you marvel at God's all-sufficiency in not needing you, yet desiring a relationship with you?
- o Have you learned to submit to God's rule over your life? To exalt God for His power and authority? To trust His providence?
- o Have you recognized God's wisdom and omniscience at work in the details of your life?
- o Does God's incomprehensibility or transcendence help you to accept the overall scheme of things (the "big picture")?
- o Has God's lovingkindness been affirmed to you through a specific situation or relationship?
- o Do you have a new respect and appreciation for God's righteous, fair and impartial judgment?

Has God brought to mind any past error in your understanding of His ways? Below, contrast any faulty pre-study thoughts and your post-study thoughts that lead you to speak rightly now about God.

It is fitting to end this study with words from the book of Job that praise our all-sufficient God. Read with your whole heart, and then write your own praise.

God…does great and unsearchable things, Wonders without number.

—Job 5:8-9

Can you discover the depths of God? Can you discover the limits of the Almighty?
They are high as the heavens, what can you do? Deeper than Sheol, what can you know?
Its measure is longer than the earth And broader than the sea.

—Job 11:7-9

Who among all these does not know That the hand of the LORD has done this,
In whose hand is the life of every living thing, And the breath of all mankind…
With Him are wisdom and might; To Him belong counsel and understanding…
He reveals mysteries from the darkness And brings the deep darkness into light.

—Job 12:9-10, 13, 22

Behold, God is exalted, and we do not know Him;
The number of His years is unsearchable. . . Can anyone understand
the spreading of the clouds, The thundering of His pavilion?
Behold, He spreads His lightning about Him And He covers the depths of the sea.
For by these He judges peoples; He gives food in abundance.

—Job 36:26, 29-31

Write a note of praise to God for how He has blessed you during this study.

Who has given to Me that I should repay him?
Whatever is under the whole heaven is Mine.

—Job 41:11

REFLECTIONS ON LESSON 12

Truths I have learned that deepen my relationship with the Lord

Day 1

What things did Job expect to hear from God that God did <u>not</u> include in His answer?

What <u>was</u> included in God's message?

What was the significance in changing from LORD in the prologue to *El Shaddai* in chapters 3 through 37 and back to LORD in the epilogue?

To what did Job admit in **40:3-5**?

Day 2

How did God challenge Job's accusations that He had been unjust in His rule of the world?

What reasons did God give Job that showed him that he was unqualified to rule over the affairs of men?

What was the significance of God's use of the object lesson of Behemoth and Leviathan?

What was Job's response to God's final challenges?

Day 3

What does Job "see" in his new intimacy with the LORD?

What were the series of reversals in the story of Job?

Why do you think that God did not include Elihu in His final rebuke?

With what did God bless Job when He restored him?

Day 4

How did Job disprove Satan's allegation that he worshiped God only for material gain?

Day 5

Discuss any changes in your understanding of God and His ways after having studied the book of Job.

As a group, present the play, *The LORD's Mysterious Dealings with Job.*

Notes

1. H. L. Ellison, *A Study of Job from Tragedy to Triumph* (Grand Rapids: Zondervan, 1958. Copyright 1958 by Paternoster), 123.

2. Francis I. Andersen, *Job, An Introduction and Commentary* (Downers Grove, IL: 1976. Copyright 1976 by Inter-Varsity Press, London), 269.

3. Robert L. Alden, *The New American Commentary: Job* (Nashville: Broadman and Holman, 1993. Copyright 1993 by Broadman and Holman), 368.

4. Ellison, 103.

5. Alden, 414.

6. John Piper, *Life As A Vapor* (Sisters, OR: Multnomah, 2004. Copyright 2004 by Desiring God Foundation), 125.

FINALE

I have heard of You by the hearing of the ear; but now my eye sees You.
—Job 42:5

Before you read and studied the book of Job, were you one who thought, "Job? Oh, that is all about Job's patience." Or perhaps this word—*suffering*—summed up your understanding. Or maybe you avoided serious contemplation altogether because, "That dialogue! It's too confusing!!" So you may have read the first two and the last chapters and declared yourself done.

When you began the study, you were given in the Introduction four pivotal questions to think about through the weeks:

Is God in control over all?

Is God just?

Is God loving?

Is God all-knowing and all-wise?

Certainly you answered "yes" to all four. But now, for each "yes," you can give solid reasons and examples, rooted and grounded in the book of Job. As you read, cross-referenced, explored word studies and answered study questions, you were gathering evidences that God is indeed sovereign, just, loving, all-knowing and all-wise.

Many of these truths have been compiled for you in this Finale. Enjoy reviewing what you know. Use the information for future studies. Pray it in praise and gratitude to your all-sufficient God.

Is God in control over all?

Although Job never knew that he was the central figure in God's challenge to Satan (Job 1:8-12; 2:3-6), he acknowledged that God had the right to rule over him (1:21; 2:10; 23:14). But he was not happy about how God chose to do so; he demanded an answer, an explanation from God (31:35). In turn, God demanded a few answers from Job. Could Job rule the world like God? No. Could Job manifest eminence and majesty to govern men? No. Could Job display power to bring down the wicked? No. After God's rebuke, Job moved from haughtiness (13:3, 15, 22; 31:37) to humility as he proclaimed that God can do all things and that no purpose of His can be thwarted (Job 42:2). Finally, he confessed that God was sovereign and all-powerful and that he, Job, was nothing (42:1-6).

This study has extolled God's sovereignty, omnipotence and providence:

- God rules over the heavens and the angels (Job 1:6; 2:1; 1 Chronicles 21:15, 27; Psalm 91:11; Daniel 6:22).
- God rules over and sets limits on Satan (Job 1:12; 2:6; Revelation 20:7-10).
- God rules over man and beast, which He created (Job 12:9-10; 41:10).
- God rules and has authority over the whole world (Job 34:13-15; 38:4-7; 41:11).
- God works all things after the counsel of His will (Ephesians 1:11).
- God keeps some of his plan "secret," but reveals other parts of it (Deuteronomy 29:29).
- God reveals much of his plan so that His children may obey His word (Deuteronomy 29:29).
- God governs the affairs of all men, including the length of their lives and position in society (Job 12:13-25).
- God demands that His children show Him honor and respect (Job 1:5, 8-12; 2:3-6, 8).
- God has the authority to equip His children to withstand Satan (Ephesians 6:10-18; 1 Peter 5:8-9).
- God has wisdom and might, counsel and understanding (Job 12:13).
- God has power over those who would defy Him (Job 9:4).
- God is so powerful no one can restrain Him or question Him (Job 9:12; 11:10).
- God does what His soul desires (Job 23:13; Psalm 115:3).
- God is exalted in His power (Job 36:22).

Is God just?

After sitting on the dunghill for a while, listening to his friends chastise him and brimming with retort, Job lamented that God was not a man as he was so that he could answer God in a court of law (9:32). He decided to "file" complaints about God, accusing God of declaring him guilty even though He knew differently. What's more, Job charged, God covered the faces of the human judges (9:20, 24, 28) and mistreated him in other ways (9:7-13). To paraphrase: "God, You know I am not guilty, but You condemn me anyway," he complained (10:7). "You know I am innocent (13:18). If You would let me argue my case before You, I guarantee You would deliver me (23:1-7). Explain why You won't answer me (30:20)! Explain why you contend with me (10:2)!"

Job reminisced about his life of integrity before he was stricken (29:12-17). To prove his innocence, Job listed to God many specific sins common at the time (Job 31). "I've done none of these things—and if I have let curses fall on me!" But Job was not really worried about curses coming to pass, so convinced was he of his integrity. No, Job was not at fault; the fault lay with God whom Job accused of treating him unjustly.

God always does right because of His character—He cannot act otherwise. If He were even one time unjust, that would mean He was flawed and therefore could not be God. Bildad recognized God's perfect justice in his rhetorical question, "Does God pervert justice or does the Almighty pervert what is right?" Elihu agreed. "Surely God will not act wickedly and the Almighty will not pervert justice." God will not be challenged about His justice; He reproved Job for discrediting it (40:8). If God had given Job—and us—the justice we sinners deserve, we would all be condemned. God dealt with Job—and deals with us--on the basis of His righteous judgment and grace.

God's justice and righteousness have been exalted in this study:

- God does not pervert justice or what is right (Job 8:3; 34:12; Genesis 18:25).
- God deals justly with those who discredit His justice or who condemn Him to justify themselves (Job 40:6-8).
- God does not need to defend or to explain His actions (Isaiah 45:7-9).
- God is faithful, just, righteous and upright (Deuteronomy 32:4).
- God, by His own testimony, delights in exercising lovingkindness, justice and righteousness on earth (Jeremiah 9:24).
- God, the Judge of all the earth, judges justly and impartially (Genesis 18:25; 2 Chronicles 19:7; Romans 2:11).
- God judges those on high (Job 21:22).
- God chooses to bestow favor on the wicked and the man of integrity (Job 21:16, 23-25).

- God is the only Lawgiver and Judge, the One who is able to save and to destroy (James 4:12).

- God hates sin and has created an eternal place (hell) for those He judges wicked and an eternal place (heaven) for those He judges righteous (Job 20:26).

- God's justice demands payment for our sins. Jesus Christ paid that price. God provided a way of salvation for Job and for us—by faith in Him, His word and His promises for Job and, for the last 2,000 years, faith in His fully revealed seed, His Son, the Lord Jesus Christ (Job 1:8; 9:33; 13:15; 19:25-26; Hebrews 11; Genesis 3:15; 6:8-22; Acts 4:12; 7:30-31; Ephesians 2:8-9; 1 Corinthians 15:1-4; Romans 3:21-16; 7:23; 10:9-10).

Is God loving?

Does God really care about His children? God's lovingkindness is rarely mentioned in the book of Job. Job acknowledged that God granted him life and lovingkindness and that His care preserved his spirit (10:12). Elihu, in 37:13, suggested that God causes clouds to form, "whether for correction, or for His world, or for lovingkindness." You have learned from your study of Job that God's mercy is sometimes severe, sometimes delayed. At the beginning of your study of Job, did you not wonder about God's lovingkindness, God's love toward Job?

This study taught that yes, God is loving. Yes, God really does care about His children:

- God mercifully restrained the power of evil, sparing Job from death (Job 1:12; 2:6).

- God's common grace covers all His creation and His special grace is to His children (Matthew 5:45).

- God exhibits providential care over His creation (Job 5:10-11).

- God does care about the details of our lives (Matthew 6:25-30).

- God is the "Father of mercies" (2 Corinthians 1:3) who comforts us (Psalm 23;4; 94:19; 119:50, 52; Isaiah 49:13-16; 66:13; Jeremiah 31:12-14) and will never leave us nor forsake us (Deuteronomy 31:6).

- God is the "Father of mercies" (2 Corinthians 1:3-4) who enables us to comfort others (Isaiah 50:4; Hebrews 13:21; 2 Thessalonians 2:16-17; 2 Timothy 3:16-17; Hebrews 4:12).

- God, in grace, provided the Advocate and Mediator Jesus Christ to reconcile sinful man to Himself (Romans 6:23).

- God sent Elihu to Job as a messenger of truth and hope (Job 32-37).

- God in lovingkindness disciplines His children (Job 5:17; Hebrews 12:5-11).

- God graciously uses discipline to open men's ears to draw them to Himself (Job 33:16; 36:10, 15).

- God forgives the repentant, demonstrated by His mercy to Job (Job 42:6-7).

- God graciously appoints intercessors and graciously answers their prayers (Job 42:7-9).

- God lovingly reveals Himself through suffering (Job 42:5).

Is God all-knowing and all wise?

In Job 37:13, Elihu acknowledged man's inability to see and know what God has hidden. However, the One perfect in knowledge performs wonders with total accuracy and with our best interest at heart. God declared about Himself in 38:37: "Who has the wisdom to count the clouds?" God's perfect knowledge and wisdom designed Job's suffering. God's plan in allowing Satan to test Job was to prove Job's motive for worshiping Him (1:9-11; 2:3-6). Job's faith endured and was proven stronger than ever as God revealed Himself through His speeches and subsequent mercy to Job and his friends.

Early in the dialogue Job declared God wise in heart and One whom no man can defy and prosper (9:4). Zophar warned Job that God knows wicked men and sees iniquity without having to investigate (11:11). Job reminded Zophar that God already has all knowledge and does not need a teacher (21:22). Elihu related that God's wisdom is exhibited in His works (37:16; 34:21). He referred to God's omniscience to expose Job's sin of rash words (of which Job later repented). He noted that God sees all of man's steps and nothing is hidden from Him (34:21-24). God's omniscience was a comfort to Job in 23:10: "But He knows the way that I take; When He has tried me, I shall come forth as gold." Job believed that only God's wisdom could explain his suffering (28:24). Being comfortable with the mystery of God, knowing that He is all-sufficient and that we won't always have answers for His dealings, we must trust Him.

The inscrutability of God means that He is incapable of being searched out and understood as His ways are mysterious (37:5). The resurrected Christ told His questioning disciples, "It is not for you to know times or epochs which the Father has fixed by His own authority" (Acts 1:7). A proper response to God's incomprehensibility and transcendence is to glorify and worship Him.

You have learned that Holy God's plan to reconcile sinful man to Himself has always been the same. Job's longing for a mediator between himself and God is our reality in Jesus Christ our Savior. The Apostle Paul called Christ the power of God and the wisdom of God: "But we speak God's wisdom in a mystery, the hidden wisdom, which God predestined before the ages to our glory" (1 Corinthians 1:24; 2:7). Yes, God really is all-knowing, all-wise, transcendent and incomprehensible. God is omniscient.

- Nothing is hidden that God uncovers; nothing is revealed that God obscures (Job 26:6,9).

- God sees everything under the heavens (Job 28:24).
- God is perfect knowledge (Job 37:16).

God is all-wise.

- He frustrates the plotting of the shrewd and captures the wise by their own shrewdness. He thwarts the advice of the cunning (Job 5:12-13).
- God judges the wisdom and reasoning of the world as foolish (1 Corinthians 3:19).
- God has the secrets of wisdom (Job 11:5-6).
- God is the Source of wisdom (Job 28:23).
- True wisdom is to fear the Lord and turn from evil (Job 28:28).
- God puts wisdom in the innermost being and gives understanding to the mind (Job 38:36).

God is transcendent.

- The depths and limits of God cannot be discovered (Job 11:7-9).
- God is in the height of heaven (Job 22:12-14).
- God dwells in the high and lofty place, but also with the humble and contrite (Isaiah 57:15).
- God's heavens and clouds are higher than we are (Job 35:5).
- The Almighty cannot be found without His help (Job 37:23).

God is incomprehensible.

- The secret things belong to God (Deuteronomy 29:29).
- God does great and unsearchable things, wonders without number (Job 5:8-9).
- God is exalted and we do not know Him; the number of His years is unsearchable (Job 36:26).
- God thunders with His voice wondrously and does great things which we cannot comprehend (Job 37:5).

> *God reveals about Himself what He wishes.*
> *Therefore, even after all of our study, we can still*
> *know only the "fringes of His ways."*

WORKS CITED

Alden, Robert L. *The New American Commentary: Job*. Nashville: Broadman and Holman, 1993.

Andersen, Francis I. *Job, An Introduction and Commentary*. Downers Grove, IL: Inter-Varsity, 1976.

The Book of Common Prayer. New York: Henry Frowde Publisher to the University of Oxford, 1892.

Cairns, Alan. *Dictionary of Theological Terms*. Greenville, SC: Ambassador-Emerald, 2002.

Calvin, John. *Sermons from Job*. Grand Rapids: Baker, 1979.

Carlyle, Thomas. "Heroes and Hero Worship, Lecture II, May 8, 1840, The Hero as Prophet, Mahomet: Islam," Public Domain.

Carson, D.A. *How Long, O Lord?* Grand Rapids: Baker, 1990.

Delitzsch, Franz. *The Book of Job*. Quoted in H. L. Ellison, *A Study of Job from Tragedy to Triumph*. Grand Rapids: Zondervan, 1958.

Douglas, J. D. *New Bible Dictionary*. Wheaton: Tyndale, 1982.

Elliot, Elisabeth. *Trusting God in a Twisted World*. Old Tappan, NJ: Fleming H. Revell, 1989.

Ellison, H. L. *A Study of Job from Tragedy to Triumph*. Grand Rapids: Zondervan, 1958.

Elwell, Walter A., ed. *Baker Theological Dictionary of the Bible*. Grand Rapids: Baker, 1996.

Garland, D. David. *JOB, A Study Guide*. Grand Rapids: Zondervan, 1971.

Green, William Henry. *Conflict and Triumph*. Carlisle, PA: Banner of Truth Trust, 1999.

Grudem, Wayne. *Systematic Theology*. Leicester, England: Inter-Varsity, 1994.

Handel, George Frederic. *Messiah*. Libretto, Part III.

Henry, Matthew. *Matthew Henry's Commentary on the Whole Bible*. Peabody, MA: Hendrickson, 1991.

The Holy Bible the King James Version. Nashville: Thomas Nelson, 1984.

The Holy Bible, New International Version. Grand Rapids: Zondervan, 1996.

The Holy Bible, the New King James Version. Nashville: Thomas Nelson, 1999.

The Holy Bible Updated New American Standard Bible. Grand Rapids: Zondervan, 1999.

Jensen, Irving L. *JOB.* Chicago: Moody, 1975.

MacArthur, John. *The MacArthur Study Bible.* Nashville: Word, 1997.

Morgan, G. Campbell, D.D. *The Answers of Jesus to Job.* Grand Rapids: Baker, 1973.

Murray, John J. *Beyond a Frowning Providence.* Carlisle, PA: Banner of Truth Trust, 1990.

Owen, John. *Triumph Over Temptation.* Colorado Springs: Cook, 2005.

Pfeiffer, Charles F. and Everett F. Harrison, ed. *The Wycliffe Bible Commentary.* Chicago: Moody, 1990.

Pink, Arthur W. *The Sovereignty of God.* Grand Rapids, Michigan: Baker, 1984.

——. *Tried by Fire.* North Little Rock, AR: Teaching Resources International, 2001.

Piper, John. *A Godward Life: Book Two.* Sisters, OR: Multnomah, 1999.

——. *Life As A Vapor.* Sisters, OR: Multnomah, 2004.

——. "The Fame of His Name and the Freedom of Mercy." Bethlehem Baptist Church, Minneapolis, MN, Sermon on Romans 9:14-18, February 2, 2003. http//www.desiringgod.org/ResourceLibrary/Sermons/ByDate/2003 (accessed August 12, 2010).

Richards, Lawrence O., ed. *The Revell Bible Dictionary.* Old Tappan, NJ: Fleming H. Revell, 1990.

Ryken, Leland, James C. Wilhoit and Tremper Longman III., ed. *Dictionary of Biblical Imagery.* Downers Grove, IL: Intervarsity Press, 1998.

Smith, Jerome H. *The New Treasury Scripture Knowledge.* Nashville: Nelson, 1992.

Smith, Ralph. *Job, A Study in Providence and Faith.* Nashville: Convention Press, 1971.

Spurgeon, Charles. *The Power of Prayer in a Believer's Life.* Lynnwood: Emerald, 1993.

Strong, James. *Strong's Complete Word Study Concordance.* Chattanooga, TN: AMG, 2004.

Vine, W. E., Merrill F. Unger and William White. *Vines's Complete Expository Dictionary of Old and New Testament Words.* Nashville: Nelson, 1985.

Ware, Bruce A. *God's Greater Glory.* Wheaton IL: Crossway, 2004.

Watson, Thomas. *The Godly Man's Picture.* Originally published in 1666; Carlisle PA: Banner of Truth Trust, 2003.

Westminster Confession of Faith of 1646.
http://www.reformed.org/documents/wcf_with_proofs/ch_V.html (accessed 8/22/2010).

Zodhiates, Spiros. *The Complete Word Study Dictionary: New Testament.* Chattanooga, TN: AMG, 1992, Revised edition, 1993.

———. *Hebrew-Greek Key Word Study Bible.* Chattanooga, TN: AMG, 1990.

Zuck, Roy B. *JOB.* Chicago: Moody, 1978.

ABOUT THE AUTHORS

Arletta Ann "Leta" Haggard was pursuing a career in clinical social work when the Lord graciously brought her to saving faith in Christ in 1985. She received a BA in Social Work from Mississippi State University and a Master's Degree in Social Work from University of Arkansas at Little Rock. She has 40 hours toward an MDiv from Midwestern Baptist Theological Seminary and Southwestern Baptist Theological Seminary. She has participated in training opportunities through Association of Certified Biblical Counselors, formerly National Association of Nouthetic Counselors (NANC) and Christian Counseling and Educational Foundation (CCEF). She is the author of the Bible study, *Fools Made Wise*. Leta lives in Sherwood, Arkansas, with her husband John, a builder. The Haggards' family includes two grown sons, Sam and Erron, and Erron's wife Beth. The Haggards served as IMB missionaries to Romania from 1997 to 1999 and as independents in 2004. They are members of Urban Harvest Fellowship (SBC) in downtown North Little Rock, Arkansas where they were active in discipleship, local ministries and international missions.

Carol Culp Robinson, who has a BA degree in journalism from the University of Arkansas at Fayetteville, has worked as a newspaper reporter/photographer in Little Rock, Arkansas, and Barrington, Illinois, and as a junior high English teacher at an American school in Caracas, Venezuela. She has been privileged to study the Bible under excellent teachers. She has received biblical counseling training through the Association of Certified Biblical Counselors, formerly National Association of Nouthetic Counselors (NANC). She has completed courses in theology given by the Ministry Training Center of The Bible Church of Little Rock. Carol has written and taught Bible lessons to women and to fifth and sixth grade girls . She has also co-authored an inductive Bible study on First John. Carol and her husband Randy live in Little Rock and worship at The Bible Church of Little Rock (BCLR). They are the parents of two grown children, Chase and Barkley Elena, and grandparents to Chloe and Eva Caroline.

CPSIA information can be obtained at www.ICGtesting.com
Printed in the USA
LVOW09s2205150415

434713LV00020B/312/P